God Is
the Answer

God Is
the Answer

Dana Gatlin

UNITY® Books

Unity Village, MO 64065

Revised paperback edition 1995

First published in 1938
Eighteen printings through 1988

To receive a catalog of all Unity publications (books, cassettes, and magazines) or to place an order, call the Customer Service Department: (816) 251-3580 or 1-800-669-0282.

The New Revised Standard Version used for
all Bible verses, unless otherwise noted.

Cover design and portrait enhancement
by Tom Hubbard
Cover portrait of Dana Gatlin by F. Tommasini

LIBRARY OF CONGRESS CATALOGING-IN-PUBLICATION DATA

Gatlin, Dana, 1884-1940.
    God Is the Answer / by Dana Gatlin. —Rev. pbk. ed.
        p. cm.
      1. Spiritual life—Unity School of Christianity. 2. Unity
School of Christianity.   I. Title.
BX9890.U5G3   1994
248.4'8997—dc20 —dc20   94-27814
[248.4'8997]
ISBN 0-87159-135-9
Canada GST R132529033

Unity Books feels a sacred trust to be a healing presence in the world. By printing with biodegradable soybean ink on recycled paper, we believe we are doing our part to be wise stewards of our Earth's resources.

Contents

Foreword 1

I   God Is the Answer 3

II   Buried Talents 9

III Dare to Trust God 21

IV   What Is the Kingdom of Heaven? 29

V   Make Room for God 39

VI   Nothing but Good 49

VII The Power and the Glory 57

VIII I Now Am True 67

IX   Out of the Rut 77

X   The Charmed Circle of God's Love 85

XI   There Is a Place 95

XII I Have No Fear 105

XIII My Victorious Spirit 119

XIV One Thing I Do 129

     About the Author 137

Foreword

*T*he following articles were written out of my own experience. When asked whether I believe in the efficacy of prayer, I reply, "Yes, I have reason to." When I first sought help from God, I was sick and discouraged, and it is through the study and application of the principles that Jesus taught that my life has been transformed. We are all children of Almighty God and inseparable from Him in whom we live and move and have our being. God is Spirit, omnipresent and omnipotent, and when in uplifted consciousness we realize our oneness, we can claim all blessings in the glad assurance that they are ours already. Outer fulfillments are bound to follow if we are spiritually steadfast. God in us is our health, our happiness, our strength, our guidance, our supply—the answer to every human problem or need.

I am grateful that these articles served to help many when they were first published in the Unity periodicals and that their message has been deemed sufficiently helpful to merit this collection in more permanent form. God can and will bless you! Rely on God with all your heart and the road will clear for you!

Dana Gatlin
Kansas City, Mo.
September 1938

1

Chapter I
God Is the Answer

Several letters from discouraged readers have prompted me to write this open message in reply. It is written to you.

This plan has worked for me: In every human difficulty, I have learned to center on God as the way out. God is the answer!

Center on God quickly, completely. God cannot fail! God loves you and is right now waiting to help you; if you really put your trust in the Divine with all your heart, God will not fail you. Utterly trusting in the Lord, you cannot fail!

Whatever your dilemma or need may be, God is the answer. You start the process of divine fulfillment in you the moment you turn to God wholeheartedly, without the slightest doubt or question. Have you been looking for help, guidance, or salvation through your own straining calculation and efforts, through some specified outside source, through some specific agency? Then you have not been trusting God utterly. You have been designating the ways and means; you have set up your personal responsibility as being as weighty as, or weightier than, God's; you have limited your vision according to your mortal eyesight and have perhaps cloaked and shut off your tremendously versatile and exhaustless resource in Almighty God.

This I have learned and should like to pass on: God is the answer! God is the answer! God is the answer! Tell yourself this over and over. Lift your head and your heart, and believe! Don't think so much about your plight. Don't scheme and fret so much regarding what you personally should do about it. Don't measure your redemption so much by this purely personal yardstick, by the yardstick of your human worries and failures and demands. You strain and wear down and don't get anywhere very much by these doggedly human processes. You are ignoring God, shutting Him out, not letting Him come alive in you so as to vivify and saturate every shred and fiber of your experience, no matter what your situation may seem to be at the moment. Nothing unlike the Omnipotent can stand against Him nor against you when you recognize that you are God's instrument. Nothing in the world can stand against that great, loving, free-dispensing Spirit of good! If only you can give yourself over to the Divine freely and trustingly, God will show you the way to gain ascendancy over every obstacle, will work through and for you, will rule you in every detail of your life—every event and deed and thought and impulse—and will rule them for good.

But this necessitates a valiant spirit of "I-trust-in-God" on your part. It means that you must give up completely your mortal doubts and fears, your thoughts of lack and hardship and limitation and of issues that you think must be met solely through the medium of personal efforts and responsibility. Let God be responsible! Let that seep into you until you become saturated with

God. God! You are of the Lord the moment you consciously let yourself be. You are not cramped or stupid or hard driven, as your self-imposed human concepts have told you. Dare to turn to the Most High intimately and confidently. Let mighty, spiritual forces awaken in you and lift you. In all things rely on God! Lose the last vestige of any sense of difficulty or shortcoming. Immerse yourself in God, nothing but God!

Try this, practice it. I don't know in just what way the loving Father of all will work in you and through you. But nothing is more certain than this: God will work! You have only to release yourself from all mortal sense of strain and admit the Almighty. The Lord will change you, change the entire color and character of your life. Nothing evil can daunt you, touch you. For you are seeing God only, relying on God, trusting God. More and more you are seeing as God sees, thinking as God thinks, acting as God wishes you to act. Almost instantly you will feel better, more optimistic and hopeful. You will look better and act better, and the outside world will note the change in you. Daily your confidence will increase and a new kind of integrity will be born. You will have new inspiration, new leading, from the Father. You will meet your tests and undertake your ventures in an entirely different spirit—gladly, enthusiastically, praisefully, with never a thought of failure, because God is your resource and guide. Your sense of God guidance will grow in you. You will be amazed at yourself, at new, unguessed characteristics and powers that quicken and come forth. Your life will take on new certainty and poise, new color and meaning. All this happens when you recognize God as the one Presence and Power, when you let nothing stand between you and Him, when you believe in Him supremely and trust Him fully.

In an issue of *Daily Word* are these pregnant sentences: "We need to keep our heart open to Him but closed to all else.... Regardless of who you are or what you are thinking at this time, turn to God for a moment and listen to His voice. If you have allowed yourself to become discouraged through listening to false voices, turn to God and listen.... Take a new lease on life. Be guided to the life of optimism and victory.... Nothing can daunt you when your ears are tuned to the song of God."

Whatever the seeming ill, discount it. Can it contend with God's power? Drop it from your attention and think of God's constant, powerful, unassailable action. Be resolute in this practice until it becomes an intuitive procedure with you under all circumstances. Put your whole trust in the Lord. Your Redeemer liveth, mighty to succor, to lift, to guide, to sustain, and to bless. Turn to God in every vicissitude or emergency of your daily life. See God rather than the undesired situation. Rely on God rather than on any prop of your personal world— employer, job, relative, or friend. One with God is sufficient to bring forth triumphant good.

Whatever the problem, God is the answer. The Lord comes forth for us when we learn to turn to Him in trust, trusting God rather than the sorry circumstances that seem to enmesh us—trusting God ceaselessly! We can be released and divinely aided. We can be lifted into the realm where we know we are secure because we are under divine dominion.

God is the answer. Thank Him. God frees us from human angers, suspicions, unruly emotions and impulses, doubts, contentiousness, the sense of human danger and pain. The Lord fortifies, strengthens, and heals us; God provides for our every need. Believe this! God calms and soothes us, works mightily to increase us in stature, sustains and guides us every moment of the day. Shut your ears to the negative clamors and know. God reveals Himself increasingly, unfailingly when we learn to abide in Him. This I know through prayer and faithful application and the vicissitudes of living: there are no human problems that God cannot meet victoriously. Your part is to put your trust cease- lessly in the Lord, regardless of outer appearances, regardless of what other people may be thinking, doing, or believing. Your part is to realize the insuperable pres- ence of the real One within you. Try the divine plan. Practice it. Hear God's promise:

> "For I, the Lord your God,
>   hold your right hand;
> it is I who say to you, 'Do not fear,
>   I will help you.' "
>
> —Isaiah 41:13

And I seem to hear you respond with quickened, glad assurance:

I am lifted into the Christ consciousness. I am one with all love (and good) everywhere. I am at peace with the world. I am free, praise God, I am free. I glorify God by allowing nothing but Him to have power over me. God loves me and tells me what to do. I trust in the Lord with all my heart. The Father of light takes possession of my soul and holds me calm and steady.

Chapter II
Buried Talents

"**F**or to those who have, more will be given, and they will have an abundance; but from those who have nothing, even what they have will be taken away" (Mt. 13:12). Perhaps no utterance of the Great Teacher has caused more puzzlement and dissatisfaction than this concise one. It is not what our human ears are avid to hear.

In the parable of the talents, the first servant had an agreeable report when his master returned, for with the five talents left in his keeping, he had gained an additional five. "His master said to him, 'Well done, good and trustworthy slave; you have been trustworthy in a few things, I will put you in charge of many things; enter into the joy of your master' " (Mt. 25:23).

The second servant also showed a gain with the two talents entrusted to him. But there was no reward for the third servant, who because of his lesser ability had been given only one talent. We can visualize this poor fellow making his wretched explanation: " 'Master, I knew that you were a harsh man ... so I was afraid, and I went and hid your talent in the ground. Here you have what is yours' " (Mt. 25:24-25).

According to Jesus' parable, the master answered: " 'You wicked and lazy slave!... On my return I would have received what was my own with interest. So take the talent from him, and give it to the one with the ten talents' " (Mt. 25:26-28).

We are apt to feel sorry for the unfortunate servant, to feel sorry for those in real life whom we see undergoing a similar experience. And how sorry we feel when something of the kind happens to ourselves. But no one has ever been so expert as Jesus in discerning the laws by which God manifests Himself in His children: "to those who have, more will be given." Often we should prefer a law more favorable to the "poor" among us, a law guaranteeing abundance because we lack, a divine law or dispensation relieving us of individual responsibility altogether—including even our responsibility to God.

But evidently this is not how the Almighty works in and for us. The master in the parable may strike us as prejudiced, harsh, and unfair. It is not a picture of the loving, generous Father that Jesus delighted to portray and all of us love to contemplate. The emphasis is not on God's "givingness" but on the rigor of a God who demands a showing, a return of His own with interest. This emphasis includes that basic Truth which underlies every aspect and every working of Truth: "The earth is the Lord's and all that is in it" (Ps. 24:1). Basically, even you and I belong to God, the great causative and working power manifest throughout creation.

God is and we are. Because God is, we are. The great Overlord has breathed the breath of life into us, has planted in us living seeds of limitless possibilities, has thus illimitably endowed us: He "richly provides us with everything for our enjoyment" (1 Tim. 6:17). But in doing this, in holding Himself responsible for us, God does not hold us irresponsible. No! In all that we are, that we do, the Lord looks after His own. You may depend on it that nothing is overlooked, not by the shadow of a hair; for the Lord, thy God, is a just God. As surely as the harvest season follows planting time, the Lord demands an accounting of all creatures, and God will be exact.

We cannot hedge with God or prevail on Him to change His dictum. Though God loves us truly, and much as He wishes us to glorify Him by prospering, God will not alter for any individual the great, splendid principle by which we exist as units in the divine scheme of life and growth. If by our own negligence, we manage poorly with the gifts entrusted to us by the Father, then those gifts automatically decrease and lessen. The law is irrevocable, and we can see it demonstrated in everything pertaining to the natural world. This very irrevocability is our greatest safeguard and protection and our greatest human hope.

We take pleasure in appropriating the statement: "All that the Father has is mine" (Jn. 16:15). Jesus Himself believed and taught this and told His followers that they should believe and teach it. "Ask, and it will be given you" (Mt. 7:7), He said. "Your Father knows what you need before you ask him" (Mt. 6:8). "Strive first for the kingdom of God and his righteousness, and all these things will be given to you" (Mt. 6:33). "The one who believes in me will also do the works that I do and, in fact, will do greater works than these" (Jn. 14:12). Jesus had no difficulty in demonstrating His ability to draw rich treasures forth from the Father's kingdom. But what He taught He practiced. When He told of what befell the poor steward who buried his allotment, Jesus was describing a type of God activity in humankind that He Himself recognized in every act of His own life. He was teaching how the God "principle of increase" works in and through humanity. He said significantly, "Let anyone with ears listen!" (Mt. 11:15) He also said, "If you know these things, you are blessed if you do them" (Jn. 13:17).

He made His point especially impressive to human ears because the thing given in trust was an amount of money. This is what many of us have chiefly in mind when we pray to the Father, who is the Giver of all gifts. The principle does apply to money, as it does to every financial transaction and every conceivable aspect of ourselves as coheirs to this green "footstool" of Earth that is the Lord's.

After rereading this parable one day, I asked myself several searching questions. What were the things I had prayed and asked God to give me? Why had many of the prayers not been answered? Was it God's fault or mine? Had I recognized all the gifts He had already given me and used them according to my fullest ability? One phrase kept rising before my mental eye: "to each according to his ability" (Mt. 25:15). Was I being fair when I envied other people because of their seemingly more favorable equipment or opportunities or their greater reward? Then the thought struck me: In what way do I deem these to be "lesser" or "greater"? For every least thing is held important in the view of the Lord. This very moment if I should honestly report to the Lord my every thought and endeavor, every deed and episode, would He answer, "Well done, good and trustworthy slave; you have been trustworthy in a few things, I will put you in charge of many things"?

What are my talents—your talents—and how are we using them?

Perhaps you will say you have little talent; materially, physically, or spiritually, you may recognize as a mere modicum the gift you possess from God. Very well, by your own claim, you are adjudged, and according to your own perception of your gift, you receive. Remember, each one is charged "according to his ability."

Let us consider what God has given you, undisputedly. God has given you life—a something so tremendous, potent, and marvelous that no scientist has ever been learned enough to analyze it, to say what it is composed of, or whence it has derived its sustaining energy or initial spark. God has given you a body machine in which to house and employ this life force, a mechanism so complex yet so accurately perfect in its intricate workings that the most ingenious human mind could not duplicate it. The Lord has given you a world to reside in and explore, a place so filled and crammed with multivaried opportunities and possibilities that all the human chronicles, records, books, and libraries known to earth are not adequate to describe it. Most important of all, most amazing and thrilling gift of all, God has given you a mind. A mind—just how would you describe this gift? It is by reason of and through the power of your mind that you know you live at all. It is through your mind, the thoughts you think with it, and the impressions you store in it that you build and are conscious of living whatever may be your experience of life. In short, your life becomes just what your mind makes it for you and just what it tells you life is.

God has given us the power to think. One of my own greatest thrills came when it dawned on me for the first time what this actually means. I had pondered the glory and majesty of God, speculated and yearned and prayed to become identified with the wonder-working God-power, and then it suddenly came to me—why, I had it—the power to believe and to choose my beliefs. This power of mental choice, of absolute freedom, and of pure, unswerving conviction was my point of union with my almighty Creator, my own, inalienable identification with God-power. With this power, I could create even as God creates. With it, I could mold and form my every thought, endeavor, and purpose as an individual; I could mold and form my aspirations and my experiences of life, my lot, my destiny. I had this power. Every moment of every day I had it. Through this power of mental choice, belief, and pure conviction, I was one with the very power of God. Words are inadequate to describe the thrill of my realization. For the first time, I beheld my own thought as something not set and static, but something alive—that brings forth fruit.

As I humbly gave thanks to the Father for this tremendous discovery, there came over me a deepening sense of my personal responsibility. I could use this living potency of my own thought, my chosen mental belief to improve every phase of my human lot to the glory of the Creator, or I could choose not to use it thus. In the latter case, what? The inner meaning of Jesus' parable then disclosed itself with such manifold angles as to include the sum total of human existence. For the first time, I comprehended God's law of increase (and conversely, "decrease"), and I saw it was not an unjust or ungenerous law, but the only method by which God's earthly children—you, I, and every one of us—might in ourselves earn the treasures that are stored in "good measure."

Any element of God's presence, God's power, God's law becomes true for you according to the strength of your conviction. Any element of God's principle works for you according to your active use of it in proportion to your cooperation. "All that the Father has is mine." Potentially, in Spirit and in Truth, yes. But I definitely have my own part to perform.

Intelligence increases with application and use. Athletes develop their muscles by exercise. It is by practice that any artist or artisan becomes perfect. It is by discovering and exercising their God-given courage, be the first-found germ of it ever so weazened and small, that cowards find themselves increasing in fearlessness. By practice, babies learn to walk, and it is by practice that spiritual infants (often adults) develop their long-hidden and often unsuspected powers. One thing is sure: you'll never get any reward from God, any increase of good, for a talent given you that you have buried.

Every time you say, "I am sick," what are you doing?

When you complain, "I am tired," you are denying and burying the elixir of life and joy that is your free gift from the Creator. When you say, "I'm afraid" or "I can't," you are burying deeper the vital germ of your fearlessness. On the other hand, every time you say, "I am not going to be sick" or "Spirit doesn't have to be sick" or "I am going to get well" or "Praise God, I'm healed with the wholeness of God!" right then, you have dug out and brought forth one of your most precious hidden gifts and nothing is surer than you will get your "increase." For nothing is surer than the action of God, who in the very life currents of your body, bestows the reward.

A chronically sick woman had often heard the phrase "since Mary lost her health" used by her family. She began studying Truth, and one day this phrase struck her ears sharply, and something within her cried, "No, you've found your health." From that day, her talent for health grew. Another woman, the victim of many distressing circumstances, in her heart kept deploring the fact that she was unable to "get back to work." One day she, too, had a sudden revelation. "No!" something in her protested. "You're going forward to work." And in her case, that is what happened. In response to her new vision of ever-widening opportunities, work opened before her, stimulating and satisfying.

A man "down on his luck" was tempted desperately to an act compromising his personal integrity. For years he hadn't even thought of God, but he spent anguished hours on his knees praying for strength greater than his own. Not only did strength come to him, saving him from a perilous situation, but his whole nature and purpose in life were changed. Incidentally, he entered upon a period of greater prosperity, happiness, security, and well-being than he had ever previously experienced. It was his Lord saying, "Well done, good and trustworthy slave."

What talent are you carrying hidden, unused? Is it a talent for vitality, for energy? A talent for love, for patience, for trust, for gratitude? A talent for industry, for diligence, for cooperation, for happiness? Are you strong enough in your innate happiness to give expression to this talent even when outer things go against you or when others tell you their woes? How great is your talent for resolution and staying power?

No thrill is comparable to your realization of increased strength through the inner workings of the Father's law, the realization that in yourself you have proved it. Unforgettable to me is the moment when I first learned I could forgive. Humanly, this often seems difficult, impossible, but it can be done! Another great moment was when I learned I could bless—not merely with the phrased words, the desire, but with the spontaneous, glad conviction of God's omnipresence—I had the power to bless. Incidentally, this realization came after I had discovered the power to forgive and after I had discovered the power to trust and to love. I honestly believe that if we spend more time endeavoring to comprehend God's integral idea of love, sincerely trying to develop this idea in our own hearts and using it in our daily practices, we should find most of our "problems" automatically solving themselves.

I have the power to believe in God, to believe in good! I have a "talent" for courage, for strength, for steadfastness, for renewal, for health. I have a "talent" for forgiveness, for faith, for confidence, for cooperation, for harmony, for love. I have a "talent" for peace, for tolerance, for poise. I have a "talent" for willingness, for service, for enthusiasm, for zest. I have a "talent" for industry, for thoroughness, for excellence, for fidelity, for success.

I have the power to see beauty; to be true to my vision, to my faith; to believe that I am guided, protected, ensured that I possess a strength greater than any I have previously shown. I have the power to express this in myself, relying ever on my Creator. As Jesus called to the latent God-life in His dead friend Lazarus, "Come out!" even so I can call to the buried God-ideas in me, "Come out!" And as these God elements within me are quickened and grow, I can give of my newfound reliance, love, and courage to strengthen and encourage others. I have the power to overcome—all my previous resistances, frictions, angers, hesitations, doubts, dreads, all my shirkings and temptations and shortcomings and imperfections and weaknesses. This was Jesus' greatest message to humankind. Jesus never made any promise of a reward to come through death; all His promises are to the living overcomer! And the accolade that accompanies each realization of new conviction, new purpose, new confidence, new strength is God's saying, "Enter into the joy of your master" (Mt. 25:21).

In Ellen Glasgow's novel *Vein of Iron*, a point is made about the human tendency to do any job only for the material reward or to do it indifferently or just well enough to "get by," without any zest for sheer excellence of performance or for doing it as well as it can be done. The sum of Jesus' teaching and of His record is a passion for human excellence in order that humankind may thus glorify the Father: "Be perfect ... as your heavenly Father is perfect" (Mt. 5:48). "All that the Father has is mine." Jesus gave assurance that our loving Father has illimitably provided for us and never withholds the lawful "increase." Protection, security, guidance, happiness, health, supply, success—the living germ of every "good gift and every perfect gift" God has put in each man's trust. Jesus explained the undeviating laws by which God works in us as we work with Him. In every detail that pertained to daily living, Jesus was about His "Father's business" (Lk. 2:49 KJV). Life, every aspect of it, is the "Father's business," but it is according to our own dutiful "busyness" that we receive, develop, and grow. Life in essence is divine activity. Inactivity is stagnation, stupor, withering, even death. "From those who have nothing, even what they have will be taken away" (Lk. 19:26).

"I came that they may have life, and have it abundantly" (Jn. 10:10), said Jesus, but He definitely declared that we must use our good gifts. By His own life, He exampled such use: Jesus believed, He knew, He served, He loved, He worked, He expected, He enjoyed, He prospered—Jesus lived His sublime doctrine to glorify the Father.

"It is your Father's good pleasure to give you the kingdom" (Lk. 12:32).

"Be perfect ... as your heavenly Father is perfect" (Mt. 5:48).

God is working in me mightily to will and to do that which He would have me do. "My Father is still working, and I also am working" (Jn. 5:17).

Chapter III
Dare to Trust God

*D*o you feel poor, sick, unhappy, discouraged? Then the most helpful thing you can do is to change the character of your thoughts. Shift your center of attention, find a new interest, something promising and compelling, something that will galvanize your mind and lift it out of its dreary rut. Change your way of thinking about yourself and your difficulties.

"But how can I?" you may answer. "That is the way things are! There is nothing pleasant in my life to think about. Everything is constantly getting more snarled and hopeless. I am at the end of my rope!"

Very well, then, give up the rope. Give up your last inch of frail, battered, unsatisfactory mortal "rope." Dare! Swing out in your thoughts and feelings. Swing out—on God.

Once when I felt sick, confused, defeated, and frightened, I found this idea of "daring" an almost miraculous help in lifting me out of my mental confusion, out of the needs and difficulties that surrounded me, over into the invisible, illimitable, infinite realm of Spirit.

Daring! Right where I am, I am daring to trust in God! I am God's child. I am daring to claim Him as my Father. I am daring to claim the unshakable Truth of all

His glorious promises. God is. God can help me! God will. I cannot describe the surge of new strength, courage, interest, and expectancy that this mere change in thought habits will arouse. Dare to swing out on the promises of the Great Unseen. Dare to claim God's life and strength and power. Dare to cast aside mortal beliefs in order to rely on God and to lean on Him only. Dare to perceive and acknowledge the Lord in the face of adverse seemings; dare to trust God through and above every situation in the world.

We cannot see God. We cannot touch Him. Therefore it is often difficult to establish and maintain our trust in God amid the adverse conditions in our lives that we can both touch and see. But this we must do, it is the one thing we must do: *trust*. My dictionary defines this all-important word as "a reliance or practical resting of the mind on the integrity, veracity, justice, or other sound principle of another person, or upon his friendship, or upon his promises as involving these; faith." Paul has defined *faith* for us as "the assurance of things hoped for, the conviction of things not seen" (Heb. 11:1). We can easily see how important and potent is the essential element of trust, which in itself is never tangible but brings about very tangible results.

Recently I had a letter from a despairing friend, in which she said: "I feel that you have proved this Truth or you could not write as you do. My own faith is not as steady as it should be, yet I must not, cannot lose it—it is all I have. Can you give me a message of hope?"

The letter moved me deeply, because it reminded me of a time when I had been in a similar situation.

"My faith is all I have," she wrote. Of course, when one has true faith, one has everything. It is out of my absolute conviction of this, gained through an ever-widening comprehension of God in my own experience, that I am writing this open letter as a "message of hope" to my friend and to all other friends who are similarly distressed.

Each person's faith is something that must be individually quickened within, and I can understand how your personal situation may have filled your mind with confusion and tormenting doubts. Yet, is all this proof that God cannot? For myself, I claim and say that God can! In any and all circumstances, I should keep on saying, "God can." For me, He has proved that He can to the extent that I maintain and develop my trust, let my consciousness be filled with His ever-present love and wisdom, and keep my faith centered in the invisible but infallible, undefeatable power of Spirit. God lives in the midst of me—with God all things are possible, against whom nothing can stand. When I think back to the sick, weak, discouraged person I once was, I rejoice and give thanks for that utter collapse. I was forced to build my trust in God, and I now know there is no need ever to be frightened again.

I have glimpsed the tremendous truth that God is omnipresent and omnipotent in every situation, waiting only for my mortal mind to perceive and claim Him, and I know that my sheer faith in divinity, proportionately as I am faithful, enables me to surmount and solve my every human "problem." In God is my trust. To cling to that trust, to increase my understanding of it, and to be true to that understanding has become my first and most important business in life.

"I believe; help my unbelief!" (Mk. 9:24) A soothed spirit, my feeling of relief, reassurance, new expectancy, was my first intuitive intimation that I had contacted my Source, that God had actually heard and was answering my prayer. God in me—in you—God in all of creation. Just what does God mean to you? Jesus taught that God, our heavenly Father, is omniscient, omnipresent, omnipotent. This means that God knows; God is here; God can. But what chance do we give this Almighty Power when we submerge It under a welter of limited, sorry impressions received from the manmade world? God gave us our mind as an individual part of the one great Mind, but left us free agents as regards how we should use it. When we cram and clutter it with the ills and adverse appearances we see around us, we not only feel very unhappy at the time but are also courting further miseries.

When we turn to God for help, sincerely seeking to know our divinity, we are not only given poignantly felt glimpses of Spirit's True Nature—the divine touch of comfort and the flash of illumination that we most need—but our mortal minds are opened to awareness of our own responsibility and power. We receive elucidation of how Divine Mind works in and for humankind, increasing our knowledge and our ability to help ourselves.

In the leaflet "Remaking Our World," Imelda Octavia Shanklin has so succinctly and forcefully explained the mind's power of creation that I should like to quote a passage here:

"The power by which we act upon the spiritual creation is the same power by which creation came. The power is the word.... The spiritual creation never changes, being the form of God's immutable word. Our world is continuously changing, being made in the form of our fickle words.

"Our world is constituted of all that we hold in consciousness, and words react upon consciousness.... When we speak a new word, our world is changed somewhat. If we reiterate the new word, the change is strengthened. A new word may have the power radically to change our world, to change it instantly. But the remaking of our world rarely is instantaneous. Our mind swings from the good that we hope to manifest and again contemplates the nongood which we hope to expel from our world.... The measure of our belief is indicated by the effect of the re-creating word. 'God said .... And it was so.' "

Don't you see why we must not, dare not, fasten our attention on distressing conditions in our outer world or fill our minds with distressing thoughts? We dare not carry around thoughts of grievance, hardship, weakness, sickness, failure, and lack. Every time we think an adverse thought, we plant it deeper in our consciousness; by our own recognition of it and belief in it, we strengthen its hold on us. We ourselves pave the way for it to become a stronger actuality in our lives. The saddest part is that in so doing we are misusing and subverting the only creative power there is, that vital, dynamic substance in us from which all things are made, that one and only power, that God-given power that lies innate in every human being, that divine power that is God in expression: "God said .... And it was so." God didn't plant sickness for us or poverty, misery, failure, and fear. The human mind thought these things, continues to believe in them, and in its personal world, continues to bring them to pass. God never thought of them, does not think of them now, and never will. As long as you or I persist in such thoughts, even God cannot help us. When we pray to God to help us, beseechingly, frantically, even God cannot do so as long as we keep our minds filled with our troubles. We cannot, dare not, carry our manmade negations to God.

Fortunately, we can drop the negations. The power of thought is humankind's greatest gift from God, and it is one of our greatest blessings that the mind can at any time change its thought and can think only one thought at a time. Instead of thinking limited, puny, wretched thoughts, we can lift our minds and think God's thoughts. It always helps me to remember that if I keep 51 percent of my thinking constructive, I am on the upswing.

Dare to lift your mind to God. Behold the Truth of God, the flawless and undeviating perfection, and have the courage to claim it as your own. If your body seems weak and sick, have the courage to ignore this mortal appearance. Let it go so that you may receive direct from God! Dare to throw away every cloud and shadow of misbelief, every evidence of manmade imperfection. Dare to turn to God and claim His glorious wholeness. Dare to say:

*I am not going to be sick; I am going to be well. I am
well right now. I am healed with the wholeness of God.*

Dare to say:

*I am not going to be poor; I am not poor now. God,
everywhere-present substance, is becoming visible in all
my affairs.*

Dare to thrill to the upspringing sense of power
within you as you make your new claim, and choose to
identify yourself with all the good that exists in the
realm of God. Try to live one perfect day in your mental
domain, one day in which you lift your mind and think
God's thoughts after Him. Say to yourself:

"I am choosing God. Today I will be true to God.
Today I will vision perfection everywhere. I will use constructively the power of my word. Today I will let my
every thought and feeling carry a blessing. Today I will
discount all my troubles and every seeming adversity.
The Lord rules my entire world, and nothing unlike God
can stand against God.

"Today I will be cheerful, generous, tolerant, patient,
kind. God neither knows nor countenances inharmony.
God is my constant companion and fills my environment. My sense of gratitude flows out and fills my
whole world.

"Today, realizing I am God's child, I will give thanks
for His protection, guidance, and enveloping love and
wisdom. I will count my every blessing and give thanks
for the countless unseen blessings that are waiting to
come into visibility. 'God said .... And it was so.'

"Today out of my trust, gratitude, and loyalty to God,
I will see only Truth and beauty back of every mortal

situation; God's ways are 'ways of pleasantness.' God-thoughts melt all the hard places out of my mind, my heart, and my world. Today I will find something to do whereby I can make life brighter and more pleasant for others.

"Today I will rejoice to know that I am a free, un-trammeled, all-forgiving child of God. I gladly give up all the thoughts of weakness and defect that have bound and hampered me—all the discontents, resentments, and frictions. I gladly give up all the hard ways. Human ways are often hard and difficult, but one way always is 'easy'—the way of Christ, leading to the glorious Truth of God.

"Today I will remember the Lord. I will turn to God and be true to God. 'He leads me.' In God is my trust."

Chapter IV
What Is the
Kingdom of Heaven?

All of us want health, happiness, and success in life. Many of us pray for God's help and guidance in order to attain them. Jesus said, "Strive first for the kingdom of God and his righteousness, and all these things will be given to you" (Mt. 6:33).

A recent letter to me from a friend asked these questions: "What is the kingdom of God? Of what is it constituted? Is it found in being kind, loving, generous? Giving our tithings to the church, attending services? Doing willingly everything that we are called to do in God's service? How are we to know if we are truly seeking His kingdom? How are we to know when we have attained that blessing?"

Millions of inspired words have been written about *the kingdom,* a proper conception of which is the basis of all Truth teaching. In the face of this, it might seem strange that so many human minds are still puzzled and uncertain about it, yet humanly, it is not strange. When I was first seeking to know God, to find the place and manner in which God's blessings are dispensed, the whole matter seemed very vague, mystical, and mysterious. Then one day it broke upon me with startling clearness! "Why, *the kingdom* is simply the state of my own mind and heart toward God—the most intimate inmost state in which I know Him and live with Him. It is being receptive to Him, the altered mood and feeling of awareness that He inspires in me. It is the state of being quickened in spirit. It is my awareness of Him in and through all the vicissitudes of my daily life."

Once I wrote an article on mental control. In it, I told of my tremendous discovery that my mind is my own domain and that I am responsible for every thought I harbor in it. Some time later it came to me that my heart is a throne of God's love. It is the deep, invisible, vital place in me where God pours Himself forth to change and enlarge my own nature—to quicken, redeem, and bless it. It is the place in me where I know God and live with God. My heart is a throne of divine love, of all mercies and blessings. There is my individual kingdom.

Jesus taught that this potent, all-important kingdom is not "Lo here! or, lo there!" that it is not in the future nor in some far-off place in the sky. Jesus said, "The kingdom of God is within you" (Lk. 17:21 KJV). He likened it to a mustard seed which when planted has within itself the power to grow into a tree; He likened it to the increasing power revealed by a lump of leaven hidden in a loaf of bread. At different times, Jesus made the following statements:

"The kingdom of heaven has come near" (Mt. 3:2).

"Search, and you will find; knock, and the door will be opened for you" (Mt. 7:7).

30

"No one can see the kingdom of God without being born from above" (Jn. 3:3).

"I am the way, and the truth, and the life" (Jn. 14:6).

"I am with you always" (Mt. 28:20).

"It is your Father's good pleasure to give you the kingdom" (Lk. 12:32).

"I do not speak on my own; but the Father who dwells in me does his works" (Jn. 14:10).

"This is the work of God, that you believe" (Jn. 6:29).

Jesus said, "God is spirit" (Jn. 4:24). God's kingdom, in the illimitable sense, is that invisible spiritual realm in which God holds, sustains, and governs the entire universe. But for you and me and for every individual, God's kingdom is simply the matter of our awareness of God as ever present. We must be born anew into this spiritual awareness. My individual kingdom is simply a matter of how much, how widely, and how intimately I believe in God, a matter of how much of God I give credence to, how much power I yield to guide and mold and control my thoughts and feelings and every experience of my life. It is determined by the state of my own mind and heart, by what I am most deeply and vitally attuned. It is determined by my conviction of God's never-failing presence, regardless of what may be happening in the world about me.

The vast sweep of God's unseen domain is beyond our mortal comprehension, but for you and me, God assumes just as much almightiness and omnipresence as we can individually sense and grasp. To each one of us, He becomes "my heavenly Father," to whom in the midst of our own being we have access and can pray. Whatever may be your conception or mine, it does not change the absolute God, the principle of all good; but to you and to me, God is exactly what we individually conceive Him to be. Likewise, His kingdom is, for each one of us, the place in our consciousness that most fully perceives God's unfailing and illimitable good.

To put it a bit plainer and in terms of everyday usage, what does God mean to you when you are sick, when someone you love is in trouble, when you haven't money to pay your bills, when you can't find a job, when you are "in a jam," when you feel unhappy, unfairly dealt with, defeated, discouraged, and weak? Do you believe that any of these outer ills, or even all of them combined, are stronger than omnipresent, omnipotent God? If so, you have allowed your own "kingdom of heaven," your own consciousness, that consciousness in which you are constantly aware of God as a living, active, and mighty Presence, to become blurred with the negative, adverse appearance of the material world. You yourself are denying God entrance into the kingdom within you.

Until you yourself believe and know and feel God there, ready and willing and powerful to aid you, your own inner kingdom will remain darkened and unavailing. As far as you are concerned, it is nonexistent, for you have not experienced it. You are the prey of many annoyances, irritations, and misfortunes. You are still wondering just where and what the kingdom is, and you do not yet know that it is waiting right in your own mind and heart.

Once I heard a man say, "The surest thing I know is that worry doesn't get you anywhere, and that as long as you worry, things won't get any better." This man had prayed himself out of sickness, failure, and many other troubles. He is now successful and one of the staunchest, most courageous, cheerful, and optimistic persons I know. For he has found God and learned how to talk and act together with God. He has found God's kingdom within his own heart, infusing him with strength daily, and he intends to abide there.

To remove darkness from a room, I must bring in the light. To remove dark and negative conditions from my own consciousness, I must turn on the light of God, knowing that this mighty Presence is in every part of my being. God is providing for all my needs. God is strengthening and equipping me to solve all my problems. God is taking care of me and my dear ones. We are held in His wise, loving arms. God is blessing my body, filling it with divine wholeness. God is in all my affairs, in my work—God's work—inspiring, guiding, and filling every phase of my endeavor.

From this wonderful place within us where we have perceived the glory of God and our oneness with the living, never-ceasing flow of good, in this uplifted consciousness that forgives, disregards, transcends, and obliterates every adverse seeming of the outer world, we find that we ourselves have the power to bless.

What is the ill condition that you have feared? What circumstances have irked you? What persons have you resisted and disliked? What false omens have frightened you? What sense of human inability has paralyzed you? Here in God's kingdom, all human ills lose their power, for what is stronger than Almighty God? You have given yourself into God's keeping; you have given over your whole consciousness. God does not sanction these earthly ills, and in the Presence within you, they vanish. In their stead, you feel the mighty tide of God-life and God-love pouring into you. You have a strong desire to let this transcendent Good possess you, to let it flow through you unimpeded, to radiate it forth from yourself, and to share it with others.

So from the happiness and gratitude of your enlightened heart, you can say to the person who has caused you anxiety: "I bless you with God's wisdom and courage and strength." To the business enterprise that has caused you misgivings: "I bless you with God's guidance and justice and prosperity." To the sick friend: "I bless you with God's wholeness and joy." To the one who has wronged you: "I bless you with God's loving-kindness and peace."

Your friends, your "enemies" (including your own ill nature and negative thoughts), your closest associates, your neighbors, the strangers you meet on the street, you can bless. Every condition and circumstance from this marvelous place within you, you can bless and bless and bless. Just try it, and feel something within you lift and soar. It is the very Spirit of God quickening within you, not by your paltry human will or your limited human strength, but by the Presence and Power released within you. "By my spirit, says the Lord of hosts" (Zech. 4:6).

As you radiate from your innermost Self the peace, love, health, joy, and plenty of God, you will feel a sense of blessing increasingly flowing from within. There are no bounds to God's blessing. Uplifted into this consciousness of your loving, ever-present, all-powerful Father, you are in the omnipresence of good. All the good in the universe derives from God, and in His kingdom, there is nothing unlike Him—no sickness, no weakness, no hatred, no inharmony, no lack. Nothing in the universe can stand against the spiritual might of God.

How clearly can you envision the Lord? How much can you feel God? How much can you experience the ineffable Presence within your innermost heart? He who created you, who gave you the spark of life, and who invisibly sustains and supports you through every vicissitude of your earthly life—how great a demand do you make on God? In your consciousness of Him as "our Father," how much of His illimitable, inexhaustible, ever-present good can you see? How much of God's invisible but unbounded and never-failing life and love and wisdom and power can you feel? How much of God can you accept, lay hold of, and incorporate into yourself? For how long can you hold to God as your one, inseparable resource? How true to God can you be?

There is nothing solemn or lugubrious about finding God's kingdom. Jesus said, "I have said these things to you so that my joy may be in you, and that your joy may be complete" (Jn. 15:11). Jesus taught that all that is required for successful living is to be derived from the kingdom of God. The vital ingredients to make us stronger, healthier, happier, wiser, more capable, and self-reliant are freely obtained from this kingdom. Not "Lo here! or, lo there!" but within you is the kingdom of God. Jesus told us that we must believe more, rejoice more, and expect more of God. Jesus said that it is the Father's good pleasure to give to us. But God cannot give when we close our eyes, when we will not see, will not take, will not be. We must be together with God, united in spirit. When we magnify the Lord who is in us, so are we magnified.

"This is the work of God, that you believe" (Jn. 6:29). Believe in what? In human inadequacies, ill appearances, inharmonies, difficulties, discord? No, that you believe in God's insuperable good. This heavenly consciousness is not always easy to attain when things of the world seem to be going ill with you. Perhaps the best way to attain it is to declare to yourself: "With God it is easy" and then to fill your mind with the sheer thought of God. "God is the one Presence and Power in the universe. He is here—He loves me. He wants me to be strong, happy, successful. He wants to fill my mind, my heart, my body, my affairs, my world. He wants to fill my whole being to overflowing with Himself so that I cannot help radiating Him to others in my every aspect, thought, feeling, touch, and deed. This is what God wants my life to be so that I may successfully express Him. Thus God wants to fill me, guide me, use me for my greatest happiness and success and to His glory. God cares; God knows how; God can! In everything I think and do, I submit myself to His great, loving presence, and He works in me for His perfect expression!"

This true thought of God will grow within you. It will develop and take possession of your consciousness in a marvelous way that compulsory human methods cannot attain. It grows of itself like the mustard seed, like the lump of leaven in a loaf of bread. Your consciousness of God, your awareness of God's unfailing cooperation in all that you are and think and do, your faithfulness in beholding the ever-present good and expecting it to "come to pass"—herein lies your own "kingdom of God" to which "all these things" will be added.

No negative thought form can come between me and my realization of God's presence in every part of my being.

I am increasing mightily in the power to express divine goodness.

I stay my soul on the mighty God and am thoroughly restored and strengthened. Father, I am here before You. Fill me, guide me, use me, work through me in Your own way, to Your glory.

I acknowledge Your presence and power, O blessed Spirit; in Your divine wisdom now erase my mortal limitations, and from Your pure substance of love, bring into manifestation my world, according to Your perfect law.

Chapter V
Make Room for God

*I*t seems that one of the most difficult things for the human mind to do is to surrender, really surrender ...

To surrender preconceived opinions, habits of thought, the *race consciousness*, personal tendencies, and reactions to whatever may be going on around us. To surrender our sense of personal responsibility, the very human tendency to think that we have to get right after every unsatisfactory condition and that we must personally set things right. To surrender our right to fret and stew and strain and tax our human strength and wits and resources to the last notch. To surrender our awareness of duties, of quandaries, of problems. To surrender our notions about the need for haste, the pressure of time—a very prevalent human notion that is a veritable tyrant over the human mind, a ruthless despot, binding and enslaving us and whipping us on and on in our heavy, dragging chains. To surrender our disappointments, our hardships, our perplexities and uncertainties. To surrender our personal prejudices about things, occurrences, and people. To surrender our very definite feelings of futility, frustration, and even despair. To surrender our emotions, grudges, and grievances; our personal conception of our duty to others and of other people's duty to us; our notion of what is owed us by other people and of how they have failed in their obligations; our convictions that things are going very hard with us and that they'll probably get worse instead of better. To surrender the seemingly incontrovertible evidence that we don't feel well, that we are sick—to surrender our disabilities, our weakness, our pain.

In fact, our minds are so taken up with all these things that are going wrong with us or with the world that there is little room left to think of God.

But we have read in the Bible that the Lord our God is a jealous God. We have read His explicit command: "You shall have no other gods before me" (Ex. 20:3).

This does not mean that the Lord is vainglorious or cruel. It means that God is all in all and that God's will for us is all good. God is supreme, the one Presence and Power, infallible, illimitable, omnipotent. But we must recognize Him. This is the law, and it is a law that we must obey. There is no evading it. The law never changes. We must change, bring ourselves into obedience to it; that is, recognize God. Then the law will work for us, work silently, harmoniously, and powerfully, and we shall cease running around in blind circles oblivious to it, wrapped up in our human struggles.

We must recognize God. It is the one demand that is made of us. But how can we do this when our attention is so taken up with other things every hour and moment of the day? These things may not please us, may plague and torment us, but our minds are filled with them; they engross us. There is simply no room for thoughts of God. How can God operate in us, perform good works, and exercise divine will in us when we will not even admit Him, when there is no room for Him in our crowded, rushing, circling, topsy-turvy thought world—a world that we ourselves have ordained and imposed upon ourselves. We may not like the conditions under which we are struggling to live—may not really like the thoughts that clutter and confuse our minds—but we are slow, loath to give them up. It may even seem, slaves to habit that we are, that we cannot give them up. So we do not. We keep on with them, though they harass and drive us. We don't rout them out. We don't clear a space for God. We don't make room for God.

Even God cannot do a thing for us when we act in this manner. He made us free agents, gave us the gift of choice. It is as if He had said to each human being whom He created: "Now, here is your mind. It is part of My Mind, indissolubly connected with it. But take it and use it. Use it, and fill it with thoughts, and remember that these thoughts have creative power that will shape and give form to your manifest life. I am leaving you with absolute control over your own mind. You may fill it with whatever thoughts you please, and if at any time you find that you have been stampeded in a false direction, onto a wrong track, just remember that you are still connected with Me. You are still a part of My Mind. Return to Me, trust Me, and I will guide you. I will never fail."

Sometimes it would seem that the Lord must become impatient with the foolish, misguided, sad carryings-on of humankind. It would seem that God must be sorry for having granted this freedom of mental action. When we forget God so completely and even will not make room for Him in the clutter of our thoughts, you would think that God might become a little angry, indignant. But God never does. God is still there, always there. God is waiting to be recognized, to be called on, waiting to help. God never changes. God never revokes His law, never fails to keep His promises. God is the one Presence and Power. God will never fail.

So it seems to me that the most important thing for us to do is to make sure that we do our part in the matter—make sure that we leave a place in mind for God, make room for Him, clear a space for Him in the midst of the human jumble. Do this every day, every time that things get confusing and beyond your human powers of direction or control. Do it even when things seem to be going well. Remember your connection with God and give thanks for God's unfailing presence and power.

It may mean crowding out some other thoughts. It may be necessary to throw them out. But this will probably be all for the best. These thoughts have probably been causing the trouble all along.

Perhaps you don't like somebody. You don't like her personality, her behavior, her point of view. She gets on your nerves. You can't possibly bring yourself to like her. Well, stop trying. But don't let your mind dwell on her errors and shortcomings. Whenever you think of her, whenever she does something that "jars on you," just try to put her out of your mind. This may seem difficult—but don't even try too hard. Just say to yourself,

"This is a good spot to make room for God." So just think of God instead. Think of yourself as establishing connection with the Divine, with God's ever-present, illimitable Mind. Don't get tense or strained over it, just relax inwardly and remember that you are making room for God. Somehow God will enter in. You don't have to bother about when or how. You don't even have to think definitely about it, to remember set phrases, or to think quickly of some manufactured, praiseful thought for the other person. You need not even force yourself to try visioning her as God's child. Just let go of her, of all thoughts and emotions concerning her. Just remember God, make room for God. God will handle the matter.

Somehow God will flow into you and do the work. You will feel the Presence, even though you can't find words to describe the activity. Perhaps another kind of thought will presently spring up spontaneously regarding the other person—God has given it to you. At all events, you will presently find yourself feeling more peaceful; and each time you practice just making room for God, you will find your private feelings and reactions regarding other people becoming more peaceful and poised. And God will guide you in what you say to them and do.

Give up the pesky little thoughts of irritation, the resentful thoughts. Give them up quickly at the moment of their intrusion. Make room for God.

Suppose you are worried and anxious about something. This is a good time to say to yourself, "Here is a good place to make room for God." Probably other human thoughts will surface to remind you that the matter is pressing, that time is short, and that you must do something about it quickly. "What to do—what to do?" It is a persistent thorn in the mind of humankind. It is a lash stinging and goading us to the necessity of acting. "What to do?" Well, try forgetting the matter as much as possible, leaving it for a while in the hands of God. This may sound foolish, illogical, and inadequate to the mortal mind; it may even sound slothful. But if you are uncertain, harassed, and driven, just try it.

Once I was writing a story that wouldn't go right. Nothing about it was going right. I wanted to write the story quickly, for I needed the check I would get for it if it sold. I needed money for many things. I set myself the task of finishing this story, for "task" it was—I wasn't getting much enjoyment out of doing it. I labored for hours each day, fighting against becoming cranky and fearful. But it seemed I couldn't marshal my ideas. The right idea wouldn't come, nor the flow of stimulation and enthusiasm that all writers of fiction know.

This element of stimulation is hard to define, but without it creative writers can do little. Some writers call it the "feel of the story." It is something inner, less tangible, yet more intimate than mere thought. It guides and propels them along a kind of track and is so alive and vital that the story always seems complete even before the job is done—so alive and vital that it compels the writer's own interest, through trial and error, until the job is done. Perhaps this element might be called "inspiration"—perhaps better, it might be called God.

I drove myself. Time was pressing. My work was bad

and steadily getting worse. I felt despair creeping over me, doubt of my abilities, but I gritted my teeth and drove ahead. I worked myself into a state of raw tension, and the story was terrible. Finally I gave up. I turned to God. "You take care of this, Father," I prayed, "take care of everything. You tell me what to do."

I tried to relax and just remember God. Quite suddenly it came to me—illogically, one might think, under the circumstances—that I should like to try writing something of my Truth experiences. I had never tried anything of this nature before. Truth was comparatively new to me, and I felt timid and humble toward such a bold undertaking. But I had been wonderfully benefited in health through the prayers of Silent Unity and through reading Truth literature.

So I began marshaling the ideas, the new lines of thought that had helped me so greatly. If I could set them down, they might possibly be of benefit to some other seeker. I became engrossed in this new work. Before I knew it, I had more than twenty subjects set down and had written five brief articles. I enjoyed the work of setting down what I had learned, the mental procedures that had benefited me, and with every page that I wrote, I felt physically better; my ideas seemed to come more freely, and my mind seemed to feel refreshed, to be clearing up.

I still felt very humble about the enterprise, but to my amazement, all five articles were accepted for publication. And here is the strangest part of it. While I was engaged in writing the articles, the idea for a story suddenly came to me, a brand-new story, and I wrote it out easily, spontaneously, marveling at the quick, sure way it was coming on. I enjoyed every moment I worked on it and completely wrote it in four sittings. I have the word of others that it is one of the best stories I ever wrote.

Make room for God. Clear a space for God in your consciousness, and God will never fail. When I first started to tithe, I hesitated, disturbed by thoughts of many material needs and obligations. Then the thought came to me: God knows no lack, no limitation. God's storehouse is illimitable, and from it, God gives freely, gladly, without end. This is the way the Lord intended us to give. God would have us give, knowing that all is from God and that the Source is inexhaustible. In that glad instant, I felt unbound and freed. I was glad to give up my human thoughts of hesitancy and calculation to make room for this revelation of God's thoughts and ways—to make room for God.

When you are harassed or uncertain, just surrender. Clear a space in the buzzing turmoil of your mortal thoughts. Make room for God. Do not even worry about what you ought to think. That will be taken care of if you turn to God in faith, trusting. You will be told what to think. The right thoughts will of themselves flow into your mind if you will clear a space for them—God's thoughts, and you will think His thoughts after Him. Try God, prove God.

When I first tried to receive healing from Spirit, I strained my mind and kept it fidgety, trying to hop from the seat of one ailment to another, trying to hold specific, good thoughts over each of them, trying to call God's attention to each of them. I did begin to feel better, for I honestly trusted God's power and willingness to help, but I was too much concerned and too anxious about narrating to God the details. Finally, this dawned on me, and I relinquished my personal hold. I surrendered. God knew—I didn't have to speak of all my ailments that needed healing. They didn't have to be healed; in God's sight, where God was, they were already healed— in God's sight, everything is perennially and eternally perfect. So I gave up the anxious strain of attention, the use of so many formal words. Sometimes I found that I was even scarcely using words, just "God—God—God." Just aware of God's presence, willingness to help, infalli- bility and illimitability, transcendent power, I let go of my anxiously hopping thoughts, gave over my personal responsibility and just left it to God. I cleared out the other thoughts and thought of God. And God came in and healed me.

I have heard the marvelous story of a little boy who was not doing very well in school. The teachers talked to the mother and recommended that he be withdrawn from the school. But the little boy had a Christian moth- er, and she prayed for him and told him of God's power to help him. The little boy believed in God's power. He did better in school. As the years passed, he stood higher and higher in his classes and graduated with honors. His formula was very simple. "When anything seemed hard," he said, "or when I didn't seem to know how, I said to myself, 'God will tell me what to do.' " And God did.

Nothing is too much for God if human beings but

give Him a chance. In so many ways—in every way, in every conceivable circumstance—it is the one sure way to help. When you have a worried thought, a harassed or driven thought, a fearful thought, a sorrowful or painful thought, a resentful thought, an unloving, unlovely thought—whatever it is, if it is of a nature to disturb you or to bring you the opposite of satisfaction and peace, let go of it. Clear it out. Remind yourself, "Here is a good place to make room for God." If you will only do this, God will certainly enter in and guide and bless you. God can. God will.

> "I will turn the darkness before them into light,
>   the rough places into level ground."
> —Isaiah 42:16

Jesus promised: "My peace I give to you. I do not give to you as the world gives" (Jn. 14:27). "I am with you always" (Mt. 28:20).

Chapter VI
Nothing but Good

At a time when I needed it badly, I received much help from the statement: *Nothing but good can come into my life, for God is in charge.*

The thought gave me comfort, assurance, a sense of security. It gave me rest and peace. It gave me strength and courage. It was wonderful to feel that God was in charge of my life and affairs and that I could overcome worry. It was wonderful to feel that God was pouring forth His good for me. I did feel that He was, and He did pour forth His good.

At that time I was endeavoring to demonstrate both health and supply, and I had made marvelous headway. In those days I thought a great deal about demonstrations. In fact, I centered upon them principally: I thought they were the main thing to center upon. But later I found out they were not the main thing.

For later I had setbacks and had to go back and do the work all over again. I had to go back to the beginning. At times I grew discouraged, but eventually I found that the setbacks made me delve deeper into the principles of Truth. They made me seek God more earnestly and led me to a closer acquaintance with God. They led me to a better understanding of the nature of

God. They led me to a different interpretation of the term *good*. I still wanted nothing but good to enter my life and wanted to feel that the setbacks were good because God was in charge, but I changed the nature of my seeking. I hope that I succeeded, at least to a degree, in changing my own nature.

The most important phase of good—the very foundation and essence of all the good that can possibly come into my life—is not some manifestation that is poured out upon me. It does not come to me through any external channel; it lies within myself. Whether or not I utilize this good and definitely exercise control over it are matters absolutely within my own jurisdiction, matters of my own volition and action.

Do I give way to a surge of annoyance or petulance? Do I feel cross today? Am I unkind to somebody or am I constrained and miserly in my show of goodwill toward someone? Do I feel moody and discouraged over my current state of health or affairs? Then no matter how zealously I pray, how can good enter my life until I do something—do my best or whatever I perceive may be done—to clear away the unlovely mental debris over which I myself have control? Even God cannot shower blessings on me until I perceive the nature of His truest, most fundamental and efficacious good, and until I do my own part toward attaining it.

Nothing but good can come into my life, for God is in charge. Nothing but good! How marvelous the promise seemed to me at first! I thought about, visualized, trustingly prayed for, and spiritually accepted in faith all the blessings that God had created and finished in His kingdom and held eternally in store for me. I believed, and I glorified in my belief. I believed in God's power and willingness, in God's divine perfection that is innate in us all, in supreme life, health, and illimitable substance—the unbounded and inexhaustible abundance of God. I liked to think of God's abundance being transmuted in various ways in the manifest world. I liked to think about successful enterprises and liberal bank accounts, about a comfortable home free from worrisome cares, about automobiles, travel, and pretty clothes.

Demonstrations occupied perhaps about 80 percent of my thoughts in my dealings with God. I made demonstrations—and then came the setbacks! Something was wrong somewhere, and finally it began to dawn on me what the trouble was. I found that a great deal was wrong and that it was all within my own jurisdiction. In fact, I found that perhaps about 80 percent of what went on in my mind was wrong, that is, not in accord with what goes on in the Mind of God.

Physical or material demonstration is not the main thing, the most important thing. We may desire to demonstrate some good, and it is right that we should desire the good, expect it, and work toward it. But demonstration of any good is always a result of something else. Something else is always the cause. Something else is the beginning. Something else is more important. When I began to perceive this, to study the principles of Truth more deeply and earnestly, new avenues of light and understanding gradually opened before me and I saw that I must change the nature of my seeking, that really I must change myself. For there was a great deal that must engage my interest and attention—yes, and my most earnest endeavor—before demonstration.

New thoughts, ideas, and conceptions began coming to me, all relating to good—God's good. I began to see that God's good—the illimitable love and harmony and perfection of Spirit—had been here all the while, was still here, always would be here. It did not change, never had changed and never would, but I had been too blinded by my very human notions of good to perceive it. I learned to be thankful that I had been compelled to change my concepts, compelled to think and realize in different terms what good might be.

I was shocked by the way in which I had blandly ignored these more vital phases of good, by the way in which I had daily ignored my own responsibility. For I did have a responsibility, a very definite one, that pertained to me solely and absolutely, which could be neither overlooked nor passed on. I could not simply leave the whole matter blandly up to God and then just sit back and rest or act as I pleased and wait expectantly for God to open the windows of heaven and pour out a blessing. At any rate, I could not do this while I secretly cherished some grudge against a fellow human being, while I passed some judgment against another or took offense or let my feelings be hurt, while I gave way to fits of annoyance or temper or indulged in moody spells or got upset over this or that, while I gave voice to my own unfavorable physical "symptoms", while I took note of misfortune—often being able to see only the misfortune—when trying to help other people in time of trouble. For while doing these things, I was not being true to God. I was not perceiving, accepting, and utilizing good and nothing but good.

Was my tone to another always genuinely cheerful and friendly? Did I share my best wholeheartedly and generously? And my "best," did it necessarily consist of money and material possessions? Something within me answered, "No." My very best pertained to me inherently, to my deepest Self—to that Self in me, cheerful, loving, patient, strong, courageous, and kind, which is established in God.

I had been so engrossed in visualizing the material blessings God was to shower upon me that I had failed to appreciate the more vital gifts or even to open my hand to receive them. I had willfully choked the avenues for God's free expression in me, without even taking cognizance of what I was doing or noting that it was my own doing.

God's good has no connection with nor anything in common with such things as ill temper, moodiness, hurt feelings, resentment, arguing, nagging, criticism or condemnation of another, or even with the imposing of personal will in the slightest degree on another. Even as it includes physical health and an abundance of material supply, God's good includes such elements as tolerance, patience, trust, poise, generosity, kindness, serenity, love, and good cheer.

Nothing but good can come into my life, for God is in charge. When we pray aright, we become increasingly aware of God's richer blessings. It is when we become sufficiently aware of them that we enter the kingdom of heaven—the kingdom of all good. It is after we are established in the kingdom, knowing its nature, that the "things" are added.

When one is established in good, one is not afraid to be generous. We wish God to give to us lavishly, but how lavish are we willing to be in our giving? How wholehearted in our kindness? Whether it be a spiritual gift of love, tolerance, and trust, or a material one, can we be sure that it is given with the full reward of generosity? Until we arrive at the point where we can be sure, our gift has not much value. God is no miser and does not wish us to be miserly. He wants us to give "good measure, pressed down, shaken together, running over" (Lk. 6:38). When nothing but good really enters my life, this is the way I must feel about every phase of my being—my thoughts and deeds and actions, my foundation in God and every angle of my human existence.

So I discovered that in giving me a new interpretation and understanding of the term *good*, God had in fact given me one of the richest gifts. God gives us ideas to enlarge our understanding; therefore, as soon as we recognize any new phase of Truth, we should adhere faithfully to our new knowledge and use it. We must act in accordance with it; otherwise, it cannot help us. Rather, because of this unused awareness, our mind will become the more uneasy and confused and things may work for us even worse than before. Be faithful— faithful to God, to every revelation. Each person has his or her individual duty to perform in the manifestation of God's good. And nobody but he or she can perform it.

"Nothing but good" means keeping alert, being earnest, persistent, patient, quick to act against subtle error habits. *Nothing but good can come into my life.* What this means ultimately is that we should be ready and quick to recognize God's presence and nature and to turn to Him, to take account of Him and His ways only. God is not short-tempered or sensitive, covetous or grasping, nor quick to take offense; God does not argue or gossip and is not subject to hurt feelings. God does not fear being dealt with unjustly. God is not discouraged or dismayed when the semblance of a headache or rheumatism or heart trouble appears or reappears, nor because a job is slow in showing up or because a particular sale fails to go through.

When I really gave some attention to it, I discovered that this matter of being true to God in my daily, hourly life was quite a business. But it is a business that can be attended to. And it must be attended to, for God not only requires that our mind be receptive, but also that it be kept free of falsity, taint, and other clutter. Being steeped in human ways, we humans, of course, find this higher fidelity difficult. But God requires that we give up every error habit as soon as we perceive it to be error. Our perception of error is really God's first step in helping us.

Everybody makes mistakes and falls down. But if we pick ourselves up and try again, we will discover that God was really helping us in allowing us to fall down. For, thereby, we have somehow gained a new understanding, a new outlook on what we are and what we should try to do. God has given us a new conception and new and truer ideas. That is how God works in revealing Himself to us.

Once I thought that demonstration was the main thing. I fell down and had to go back to the beginning—and that was good. It is always good, for "in the beginning God ..."

I had not learned fundamentals or else I had ignored them. Take care of the fundamentals, and demonstration will take care of itself.

Nothing but good can come into my life, for God is in charge is still one of my favorite prayers. It gives me so much peace, assurance, strength, courage, and a sense that all is well. But the principal reason I like it and give thanks to God for it is that it has been the medium through which I have come into a constantly enlarging comprehension of what is meant by "good." Nearly every day a new viewpoint challenges my attention. I am taught to alter my point of view, my behavior, and to be on guard anew. I am given wisdom to understand and strength to abide by every new revelation that comes to me. I praise and give thanks to God for having given me this prayer: *Nothing but good can come into my life, for God is in charge.* As one tries to remember it, to abide by it, to understand and apply and live it, there seems no end to the new grains of understanding one may glean, until one shall finally arrive in the kingdom itself and truly know God.

I know that God is the omnipresent good, and that God occupies, as the Spirit of good, every part of my being.

Chapter VII
The Power and the Glory

*F*or the kingdom and the power and the glory are yours forever" (Mt. 6:13).

These familiar words have become empty phrases to many of us. If we are worldly-minded, we are used to deeming them superstitious, impractical, useless. Even if we are "believers" eager to prove our connection with the mighty God, these words from Jesus' own prayer are apt to seem mystical, mysterious, pertaining to something detached from us, something strange and far away. Jesus said plainly, "The kingdom of God is within you," and He promised His followers that if they found this invisible kingdom within themselves, all the "things" they desired would be added. But this instruction doesn't always help us. We can all ponder on the tremendous, universal power that is God. What is more difficult is to identify our human self and everyday experiences with this power.

Jesus taught that "God is spirit," the Giver of life and of all that life holds and connotes. You cannot see God but neither can you see a current of electricity or the life force within yourself that causes your heart to beat. Even though you are an utter materialist, you cannot deny the existence of life and love and wisdom and power, for you see evidences of these about you all the time, and doubtless you wish that you yourself might find greater access to them. There is a way to do this, the Jesus Christ way. And right where you are is where it is to be found.

Jesus avowed that His mission was to teach human beings to live a fuller, richer, more successful life, "I have said these things to you so that my joy may be in you, and that your joy may be complete." Jesus did not pray to God now and then, merely in emergencies, on specific occasions, or in some specified spot, nor did He address set phrases to a remote and mysterious deity. In every moment and deed of His life, Jesus lived with a sense of inseparable union with the unseen Almighty Presence, "I do not speak on my own; but the Father who dwells in me does his works."

I in Him and He in me—wherever I am, whatever I am doing. Most of us do not live intimately enough with God in the pursuance of our everyday tasks, hopes, and endeavors. Listen to the promises: "The kingdom of heaven has come near." "For everything is ready now" (Lk. 14:17).

What is it you want from God to become manifest in your life? More health, more happiness, more wisdom, more prosperity, more success? You want assurance, strength, guidance, do you not? Then take it. Say to yourself: "God is here, filling me, filling my life and my whole world, and I mean to have Him. I mean to be one with God who is the essence of all good, with whom all things are possible. Nothing external or adverse can stand against God! Not even my own weak, warring

human thoughts, no seeming difficulties, no outer circumstances that disturb or jar."

When you acknowledge to yourself that anything in
the world is too much for you, that certain conditions
or persons are the cause of your trouble, you weaken
yourself in your own estimation and certainly weaken
yourself in the estimation of the world. And much more
important, you are denying the omnipotence of God
and are shutting Him out of the only way in which He
can help you.

Jesus said that the kingdom of God is not "Lo here!
or, lo there!" but "within you"—in the minds and hearts
of men, in your heart and mine, the place where we
perceive and partake of and radiate forth the power and
glory of Spirit. God in the midst of me is mighty, here
and now, wherever I am, undergoing whatever experience of life—mighty to fill me, to change and restore
me, to develop the highest forces of my nature and, if
needful, to change my nature; to make me stronger,
wiser, and more capable than I was before; to use me, to
guide me, to lead me into victorious, happy, and successful living.

We all want good. Usually we look to the outside for
it and anxiously plot and plan ways and means that will
serve our interest. But this is not the sure way, the Jesus
way. "Do not worry about your life" (Mt. 6:25). "Your
heavenly Father knows that you need all these things."
"Knock, and the door will be opened for you." Even
when we turn to God, eager to receive, we are apt to
concentrate on the method. How is God going to work
this out and bring it to pass? What steps does God want

us to take? Just what does God want us to do?

God wants you to do these things: to recognize Him; to feel Him near; to admit Him into every recess of your conscious being, into every act, enterprise, and endeavor, into every corner of your mind and heart; to unite yourself and your whole being with the Lord, trusting God utterly for support and guidance; to incorporate yourself in God, the great unseen Spirit without which nothing is made manifest; and to know God is here, in you, and in everything everywhere, desiring only to pour forth His illimitable good.

In every phase and circumstance of our worldly experience, we must be aware of the unseen but powerful Presence. In our minds and hearts we must behold God, love God, rely on God. Our consciousness must be filled with God—first inwardly, then outwardly. Our whole consciousness must expand and quicken with the glad knowledge of the presence of God. When we really come to know God and to thrill to His quickening Spirit of life and love, our good has already come. Our attention no longer strains toward outer anxieties and frets and ills. A great peace comes upon us; we feel Him near, feel Him filling us. God cares; God knows how; God will guide us infallibly in everything we think and do. This peace in us is our own intimation, ever deepening and widening, that the almighty, overall Spirit is working in us.

The consciousness of God's presence within you, of your union with the unseen but mighty Presence, gives you augmented strength, courage, and purpose to meet the daily demands and vicissitudes of life. If you are in doubt, in perplexity, under stress, in any trouble, just try it! Simply toss these seeming ills aside, and begin to say to yourself—and feel—from the bottom of your heart:

God-power right now is strengthening, helping, guiding, blessing me. God-power is now flowing and finding expression through me. I have claimed it and taken it for my own. God-power is now released in me, is changing that in me which needs to be changed, is bringing forth the highest forces within me. I expect strength from God-power only; I rely utterly on God-power. God-power is now in action in me—is acting now—to serve my needs and to fulfill my sincerest, highest desires. "I do not speak on my own; but the Father who dwells in me does his works."

Right where you are, this power is to be found. You do not even have to strive for it; just keep expecting, glad and confident and thankful. Not your mere human power but the very power of God, mighty to augment your own, to build you up so that you may be better equipped to meet and master every human situation.

Your consciousness of God is something that you can carry with you everywhere you go. God never forsakes you; it is you who forsakes God. What is it you most need and desire from life? Jesus said, "Strive first for the kingdom of God and his righteousness" (faith in the orderly outworking of good). And how do we find the kingdom? Why, by believing, by knowing it is there. Within yourself, you have access to the full glory of God, to all that you can lay hold of. All the life and love and wisdom and power you can conceive of are invisibly waiting, ready to pour forth in you, to transform your mind and heart, your very nature, your whole being, your experience, your entire world. According to your *consciousness* of God, of His presence, love, willingness, capability, and power, your own "kingdom" will be measured and defined for you. You will know when you have found it by your increased sense of love, trust, guidance, and peace.

Just what does God mean to you? You cannot ask this of yourself too many times. How high is God to you and how close? How mighty and how bound into your very being with tenderest love? How merciful, how loving-hearted, how strong, how able, and how wise? Is your mind filled with anxieties, hardships, failure, criticism, mistrusts, suspicions? Then you have left small space indeed for your own heavenly kingdom. These unlovely entrants are not of God, from God, nor true of God. To benefit from God, you must choose Him and lay hold of Him. Any of us can make our own choice at any time. If we like our turmoils and failures, we can continue to live with them. If we want something better, we can make a change.

We keep ourselves blinded with too much human beholding. We are sick or out of a job; people are unjust or unkind to us; we are convinced that we are having a very hard time. We may try to pray, but it doesn't seem to help. For even in our prayers, we keep our attention on our ills, straining for evidences of improvement. "Faith is ... the conviction of things not seen" (Heb. 11:1). We keep looking outward for the answer without being utterly, unreservedly, steadfastly sure of God. We seem reluctant to concentrate on God's divine goodness and to let the great, loving Spirit fill and expand and uplift and impregnate our own spirit. We seem unable to feel God dynamically, ineffably close, while we gladly, consistently, and confidently do our best in our outer occupations day by day, moment by moment. The answers will come. Don't doubt it. How? That is not for you to question. God's ways of manifesting divine goodness are more numerous than the leaves in spring or the sands of the sea. God knows how to bring good into visibility. Your business is to keep yourself an open channel, to feel divinity near, to give thanks and rejoice, to cease giving importance to the unlovely conditions that you don't desire, to behold God and to expect more from God. Your business is to train your innermost heart—whatever the outer conditions—into the feeling of being with God.

God knows how to strengthen, to develop, to guide, to improve—yes, how to alter and improve even the stubborn impulses of my own human heart. Straight from the heart of God—into my own heart. All that God has is mine, unseen but in the very heart of me, according as I perceive, lay hold of, and become a part of His sublime goodness. My own heart, my whole being—yes, my whole world—is beautified, enriched, and blessed from this feeling of togetherness with God. Nothing external can prevail against this supernal region of good. Nothing is comparable to this marvelous feeling, this transcendent union with "our Father" whereby I am augmented with strength, wisdom, love. God in the midst of me—*in the midst of me*—is mighty. This is the place in which I am empowered to will and to do those

earthly tasks and deeds which heretofore seemed difficult, impossible. This is the hidden, wonder-working
spot of small improvements and of miracles. This is the
place in each one of us where God does mighty works.

God does mighty works, not by my mere human
power but by my power enhanced by God's power; not
by my limited, blurred human perspective but the
undimmable sweep of vision; not by my human difficulties, entanglements, failures but God's all-embrac-
ing, ever-present wisdom; not by my conflicts, temptations, dislikes, condemnations but divine love, infinite,
wider than the heavens, closer "than breathing, and
nearer than hands and feet"; not by my hardships,
griefs, sorrows but the infolding Spirit of peace and joy,
radiant as the morning sun and as accessible as the air
we breathe; not by my heart—troubled, fearful, or dis-
eased—but God's heart manifest even in me and
attuned to the glad, sure rhythm of the universal pulse;
not by my hands, incapable, weak, or unwilling but
God's hands made visible in my flesh, tireless and gifted
with the very endowment of God; not by my ability, my
work, my affairs, my life—but God's.

Remember this. According as you expect and consciously lay hold of, you set power in action. Do you
say: "I can't," "I don't see how," "I'm afraid"? Then you
won't be helped by the waiting, ever-ready power of
God. Within you, you have that divine power. The
power to bring forth divine good, to unite yourself with
God power! You have the power to ignore evil and
weakness, the power to forgive, the power to think and
feel and live constructively, the power to spread happi-

ness and well-being, the power to behold God working in your enterprises and in your fellows, the power to do a distasteful job well, the power to find a job, the power to be healthy and dauntless and strong, the power to help and bless others.

"For the kingdom and the power and the glory are yours forever." It is in this uplifted, jubilant consciousness that you behold the kingdom of God. Not "Lo here! or, lo there!" but in the "secret place" within yourself, where you recognize your unseverable relationship with "our Father." "Your kingdom come. Your will be done, on earth as it is in heaven" (Mt. 6:10). It is from this marvelous inner beholding place in ourselves that the great, loving Spirit pours forth to change our misguided human thoughts, to upbuild our inner life to loftier stature, to bring forth peace and joy and success in us, to transmute our whole being, and to transform our entire world.

"As You keep the stars in their courses, so shall You guide our steps in perfect harmony, without clash or discord of any kind, if we but keep our trust in You. For we know You will keep him in perfect peace whose mind is stayed on You, because he trusts in You. We know that, if we acknowledge You in all our ways, You will direct our paths. For You are the God of Love, Giver of every good and perfect gift, and there is none beside You. You are omnipotent, omniscient, and omnipresent, in all, through all, and over all, the only God. And Yours is the kingdom, and the power, and the glory, forever. Amen."

Chapter VIII
I Now Am True

The Prayer of Faith

God is my help in every need;
God does my every hunger feed;
God walks beside me, guides my way
Through every moment of the day.

I now am wise, I now am true,
Patient, kind, and loving too.
All things I am, can do, and be,
Through Christ, the Truth that is in me.

God is my health, I can't be sick;
God is my strength, unfailing, quick;
God is my all; I know no fear,
Since God and love and Truth are here.
—Hannah More Kohaus

We may entertain a certain thought or use a certain statement over and over without grasping what it really means. We may think we comprehend it fully, but then suddenly a deeper, more vital, more compelling meaning strikes us, and the result is electrifying. It is as if we had never even remotely grasped the meaning of the words before.

It was so with me one day when repeating "The Prayer of Faith." Every statement in the prayer is so beautiful, so comforting and strengthening that I have always loved to ponder the phrases and steep myself in their wonderful promises and assurances of security, love, and peace. I thought I had grasped their full message. But as I repeated the words, "I now am wise, I now am true," I was arrested suddenly as if by a flash of blinding, white light.

"I now am true"—just what were these words I was saying? Just what kind of responsibility was I assuming? What kind of obligation was I putting on myself? And it came to me suddenly, in that brief, vivid blaze of revelation, that this was really my only responsibility, that it was the only obligation God would ever put on me, and that if I faithfully fulfilled my part in this matter between God and myself—if only I were true—God surely would take care of everything else.

Everything! No matter by what adverse aspects I was seemingly surrounded—sickness, pain, inharmony, depression, poverty, failure—it came to me sharply that these were merely opportunities to prove the Truth, that they were false ills, to be routed simply by my being true.

The simplicity of it was what electrified me. The complexities of life, the endless, interwoven ramifications of my obligations both to my personal world and to God had put a strain on my attention and had bewildered and frightened me. But now, in that one brief flash—oh, so simple, so blessedly simple!—it was as if I had encountered a signpost in the dark and confused strivings of my own mental world. Here was something to steer by. Four words out of my own thought would always bring me back sharply whenever I should get lost or stray: "I now am true."

Of course it put the proposition squarely up to me. And the proposition still held its innumerable, interlocking human ramifications, but under that blazing flood of illumination, I felt a thrill of strength and purpose such as I had never felt before, a thrill of thanksgiving to my Creator for displaying my sole responsibility to myself in terms so unmistakable, forceful, and clear.

"I now am true." True to what? Why, true to God of course!

When I doubt God, I am not being true. When I doubt God as the Supreme, the One and Only Power, I am not being true. Nothing can stand against God. The Lord simply is. In the midst of the wide, variegated creation, God is divinely unaware of small, personal angles and tangles and jangles. God is aware only of the glory and perfection of creation. The Almighty beholds it operating smoothly, easily, perfectly, a process infinitely simple and ordered throughout its infinite multiplicity of operations. God takes no account of any disorder, discord, or confusion. There is no possibility of this where God is. "With God all things are possible" (Mt. 19:26 KJV), but with Him there is no possibility of the slightest inharmony, the least weakness, the faintest disturbance or doubt, or anything that in any way deviates from His divine institution of what is eternally

69

adjusted, glorious, good, full, and free. God stands in the midst of creation, ruling easily and effortlessly according to the steady, undeviating, unbreakable laws of harmony, completeness, and all good.

When I begin to suspect that there may be something in this world that can stand against the power of God, I am not being true. When I doubt that anything in my experience of the manifest, human-directed world is essentially "good," I am not being true. I, and others about me, may have worked havoc by our human misconceptions and our misoperation, and certain appearances may, of course, result that are far from satisfactory. But these are merely distorted effects that engage and disturb my human attention, that fill and disturb my human consciousness. They do not engage or disturb God's attention. In God's consciousness, they do not exist. With God, all that exists—creation and the operation of creation—is good, unassailable, and complete—nothing but good. With God, there is simply no question of anything else. Everything is good and functions gloriously, smoothly, and well.

God exists in creation—in you and in me and in everything that may ever happen to, in, or around us— as the omnipresence of good, not as anything evil or menacing or disturbing or frightening or ugly or weakening or painful or imperfect. None of these things— no! He is the omnipresence of good. All good, already created, the full glory of all good, which in our human natures, you and I can scarcely perceive, yet which is in you and in me, functioning for you and for me. Anything contrary to this God does not countenance.

God is the omnipresent good in creation, and as the Spirit of Good, occupies and rules every part of our being.

This is the way God views creation, the way God views you and me. If you and I view ourselves differently, if we view the things that happen to us or around us in this mortally manifest world in any way that God would not view them, then we are not being true to God.

God is the omnipresent good, and as the Spirit of Good, occupies every part of my being. Think what this means. God knows this Truth, recognizes nothing opposed to it, but wants me to know it too. He wants me to know and believe and feel it and live it and manifest it in every department of my being. More, God *demands* that I know, believe, feel, live, and manifest it. This is the only requirement Spirit makes of me, that I recognize and accept this omnipresence of good—I in God and God in me—ever and beyond and despite any seeming limitations of the sense world. If I recognize and accept the Spirit, if I see and honor God as the infallible, illimitable, infinitely ordered omnipresence of good in my life, and if I regard anything else as of no account whatsoever, then the Spirit will come forth in me and manifest the fullness of good even in my mortal life so that I shall not have room enough to receive the blessings.

But I must be true—true to God, true to my revelation and acceptance of God. In the face of repeated false seemings, I must be true. The false seemings are the results of misguided, willful, human conceptions that did not have their origin in or authority from God. If they are in any way imperfect, inharmonious, weak, or ugly, they have never had any existence in God, do not exist now, and will never exist. They are but the fruit of man's distorted imaginings, his human perversity and willfullness. They are ugly clouds of unhappiness, dissatisfaction, lack, strife, and pain. No one really likes them very well, the misfortunes and struggles and trials of the human-managed world. But there is always one thing any one can do—the only thing to do: Remember that in God's sight they do not exist, that God's creation is ordered, perfect, and that in it, God rules supreme.

"But how do I know that God will bring perfection into manifestation for me?" you may ask. "Everything around me is chaotic and wrong. Nothing is right. I am sick, I am poor, and I am unhappy. How can I just throw these things away when they constitute the very fibers of my life?"

If you ask such questions as these, you yourself have given the answers as to why you should throw them away—because you have made these imperfections the very fibers of your life and have woven them into a structure that is neither reliable nor pretty; you must somehow manage to throw them away before they destroy you. You must find the courage simply to toss aside, as of no account, every condition and phase of your life that fails to measure up to the standard of "omnipresent good" and come empty-handed, as it were, to the throne of God.

"Here I am, Father," you will say. "All that stood between us I have thrown away. They were sorry things, but that no longer matters. All those fallings short, failures, dissatisfactions, and troubles are gone: they do not count a whit. I know that You are the omnipresent good, that You will help me and show me what to do. I of myself can do nothing, but I know that You will instruct and direct me. I rely solely on You; from the bottom of my heart, I am relying on You. There are clouds and shadows still behind me, but I have turned my back on them, for I know that for You, they do not exist. I know that in Your creation all is prepared and ordered and that You have a bright, clear path for me to follow. Show it to me, Father. See, I have come empty-handed. I put my whole trust in You."

If your longing is sincere and your heart is true, God will not fail you.

In reality, God never fails. God cannot fail. It is only you yourself, in your misconception and your failure to trust, who can ever fail. When you recognize this fully, you will accept God fully, and your life will be transformed. God knows His own power, but before you can build your earthly life around it, you yourself must know it. Even though the most adverse appearances seem lined up against you, you must be able to say from the bottom of your heart: "These things do not matter a whit, for they are not true of God. God will shine through them and dissolve them as sunlight dissolves shadows. God is in charge in the realm of Spirit, and nothing can stand against God. My trust is in God. Spirit will tell me in plenty of time what I of my human self should do."

Does this seem far-fetched? Does it seem too vague,

lazy, and lackadaisical? Yet it is not vague. It is the only way that the human mind may rid itself of its insufficiency and lift and merge itself with the Mind of God. It often requires much courage for the human mind to cast off its human props in this fashion, but when you have become absolutely true, you will know that you are taking no risk. You will know from the depths of your being that of yourself you can do nothing, but that "with God all things are possible." You will gladly drop your doubts, confusions, inadequacies, and hesitations so as to let God through. You will thrill with the knowledge that God is in charge. With that thrill of joyous conviction, you will say, "God is—God can—God will!" When you feel the power of God working in you and prompting you, you will find there is nothing lazy or lackadaisical about it.

God rules. When you are true, you will know this; you will not for a moment believe anything else. You will not fret and waste your energy trying to imagine how He is going to help you. Some time ago Jan Debonheur in an article in *Weekly Unity*, "Prove Me," put this point so clearly and forcefully that I should like to repeat it:

"Suppose your house is burdened by a mortgage, suppose you have no idea where your next meal is coming from, suppose you are suffering from what the world believes to be an incurable disease. If you can say, 'Father, I thank Thee that it is done,' from the bottom of your heart and accept your good in place of the seeming evil, then the Red Sea before which you are standing will divide and you shall pass over safely.

"Never mind how—do not try to imagine how. More manifestations of good have been held up by the 'hows' of the human mind than by anything else. You don't have to question the law. 'I am the way.' 'Prove me.' "

If I am true! How then, after I have glimpsed the Lord, when I have felt God, have listened to God's promises, can I ever be false in my human feelings or words or deeds or most secret thoughts? How can I ever let my mind be tormented and my spirit stung by any outer event or circumstance? By strugglings or disappointments? By weakness and pain? By fears, janglings, contentions, resentments, condemnations, and spites? Such ugly turmoils have no place in God: they are not even remotely connected with the "omnipresence of good." But if I clog my mind with them, clog my life, I am devoting myself to something other than God. I am willfully cluttering and blocking the channel through which I receive my help. In such case, how could I expect to receive the blessings for which I have prayed? The trouble with the majority of us, even when we pray, is that we give so much attention to our ills, problems, and trials that we pay scant attention to God and the laws of God. Or thinking we are sincerely praying, we keep our attention strained on the effects, the material results that we desire. We want God to rule our material world, without letting Him rule our spiritual world. This cannot be done. It is in Spirit that we are children of God, and all is harmonious, perfect, complete. The spiritual world comes first. It is there we receive the blessings that have already been prepared for us. We must learn to abide there, to abide the coming of our

Lord. He will certainly come if we are true, and if we are true, the blessings we desire will certainly come forth gloriously for us in our manifest life.

"Not by might, nor by power, but by my spirit, says the Lord" (Zech. 4:6).

My life is centered in the Spirit within me, with Christ in God.

God is. God can. God will!

God is the omnipresent good and occupies, as the Spirit of Good, every part of my being.

My life, and everything entering my life, is a glorious, completely harmonious, and infinitely ordered thing of beauty, under the direction and control of the one divine Power.

I now am true! I have faith in God, faith in my neighbor, faith in myself.

"Father, I thank You for this light that You have given me by which under all earthly circumstances I may be guided. I thank You for Your living presence and for Your promises that are eternally true."

Chapter IX
Out of the Rut

*A*re you in a rut—mentally, physically, or by force of material circumstances? Do you wish that some lucky event or benevolent person would come along and pull you out? Do you wish you could pull yourself out, up to greater efficiency, happiness, and success, but don't see how? Well, you can. There's a way you can pull yourself out of any kind of rut that exists in this workaday world.

You may think that your limited surroundings or that certain conditions are at fault. But no outer condition need have any influence on your happiness and achievement. Within yourself, you have the capacity to be stronger, bigger, surer than you have ever been before. The day I made this startling, invigorating discovery, the transformation of my life began. I can now feel only gratitude for the seeming afflictions that turned me despairingly to God, for all my life, theretofore, I had felt dependent on outer props and circumstances for my help.

One day I was feeling tired and discouraged and wishing that things might turn out more happily for a while. I had been thinking of my problems, of the changes I should like to bring about, of the duties and tasks for which I had no liking or strength, and gradually I began to think of God, to whom I had so vainly prayed. Just who and what was God? I imagined, "Just what would He do to start setting things right for Himself were He here right now in my human place?"

These inner experiences are hard to describe. But while I sat envisioning God, so to speak, taking charge of my personal situation as if it were His situation, a flash of illumination penetrated my jaded, inert mind. Would God be sick, despondent, and weak with vain wishing? No! God would be strong, confident, competent. God would think, would act, would do.

I felt as if something inside me had been under the manipulation of an expert masseur. It must have been a direct renewal of my spirit, for eagerly, conscious of no effect, I began to plan courses of action that would lift me from my mental rut. I could hardly wait to get at some of those tasks, which a short while previously had seemed arduous, tedious, disagreeable, and some of them intimidating. For this is often the reason hidden back of our sluggishness and failure to act: fear. Oh, the surface of our mind puts forth all kinds of excuses, but the recesses of it have shrunk down into their ruts because they are afraid to rouse themselves and try for something better. Instinctively, we are afraid to try again because we are afraid we'll fail again and get hurt again!

But now as I pictured God sitting in my human place, as it were, something inside me was jolted from its lethargy, galvanizing it into new resolution. It was as if someone spoke: "Act as if you are a child of God. Let God act in you. Can God fail?"

Remember, God is living energy to quicken, increase, and guide our own energy. Spirit is a living elixir to lift, sustain, and establish our own spirit.

We can get in a rut even when we pray. We ask God to work miracles for us while we sit not very hopeful or stew in our own juice, impatient or resigned. In our daily efforts, we drudge too much in the drab mood of duty or repining. It takes all the life and spirit out of us even though we are inclined to be a bit proud of duties painfully performed, a bit proud of being martyrs. But that's not God's way of doing things. God doesn't love a martyr—a weak, timid, cringing, complaining soul. God doesn't love joy killers, joy evaders. Of course this statement isn't strictly true, for God impartially loves everybody. But God cannot infuse Himself as life, power, and joy into the person who denies and cuts God off. We can never benefit fully from God's love and wisdom unless we feel and act as if we are a part of Divinity. God is able to give us every good gift, to enrich our lives and to aid us in every earthly enterprise. When we won't recognize and take the gift, then we must do without it.

Often we are held back by our doubts, and often we make too much of an effort to trust God. We seem unable to take God—Good—for granted simply, to take God spontaneously and naturally, as we take our heartbeats and the air we breathe. It seems difficult to accept the Lord with certitude and unquestioning, native joy. If you were positive that some great good was about to come into your life, what would be your inner feeling, your mood? This inner attitude or state of feeling is analogous to that greater, transcendent mood of absolute assurance and joy that colors your entire being when you feel yourself to be a part, a living expression, of God, of All-Good.

Do you want to be more successful? Are you in the rut of nonsuccess, and do you want to lift yourself out? There is a way.

Suppose you were out of a job and God should go forth to seek the job in your stead. Would He be able to get it? Would God show the same qualifications that you are showing? If not, how would they be altered? Suppose God were sick; could He make Himself well? Suppose God had to perform a difficult or a distasteful task or was placed in the midst of inharmonious surroundings. In any situation you can imagine, you can imagine God there and how He would act. And remember, God is waiting to act through you. Do you imagine that God would not be able to control His temper or that He would slack up and show poor, demeaned abilities or that He would get frightened and scurry away from a spectacle of human distress or that He would complain bitterly about a seeming injustice or feel sorry for Himself or lament, "I don't see what on earth I am going to do"?

No! That is not how any of us envision God. Nor is it how we should envision ourselves as the children, each of us a living expression, of God. In our daily habits and enterprises, we don't live sufficiently in the expectancy and mood of God, of Good. Even if we were positive that some great good was about to come into our lives, we do not seem certain that we should be in the mood for it.

Get out of the rut! Cease believing in what isn't good, in what is weak, inadequate, futile, in what doesn't measure up to God. Get out of the rut of sickness, difficulty, inharmony, insufficiency, failure! Our minds, which think so ceaselessly and insistently, are the most marvelous instruments imaginable, but it is up to us to control them and to choose the kind of thoughts we think, to train ourselves into courage, real efficiency, and stability. Even more difficult to control are our moods, emotions, and attitudes, which are so intangible and undefinable but which are such potent factors in determining our experiences of life. Yet we can reduce these to simplicity. When children are going on a picnic, they act happy because they feel happy. They feel happy because they are facing a definite, pleasurable experience. This is the way we should feel within, innate and bubbling and spontaneous, at every moment and in every undertaking of our life because we are facing God, the good.

God, the good, in me, with me, for me—in, with, for everybody, everything: everything I think, do, see, or feel is simply a part of God, of Good. Why should I feel hopeless or unhappy? God isn't hopeless or unhappy, is He? Why should I or anybody else be sick? Almighty Spirit is not sick. Why should I be angry, impatient, short-tempered? This is a state where my feelings are concerned, and I can't be any of these ugly, undesirable things if I am engrossed with the glorious sensation of being a part of God. Why should I be suspicious, hesitant, doubtful, shrinking in my hidden, innermost nature? Why, I can't be if I am intimately interwoven with the very nature of immanent, omnipotent good, if my moods and feelings are of the very same stuff and substance that constitutes God. Why should I feel anxious, uneasy, or inadequate, or fear that I might fail? Does God fear for the success of His enterprise? Does God shrink, tremble, grow paralyzed, or faint? No!

Fearlessly, let go of them: all the little bothers, the irritations, the jealousies, the dislikes. Do not give them any room in your mind. Let go of your disappointments, your sense of inadequacy, of discouragement, of failure. It does you no good to harbor such feelings. You only weaken yourself more and more. You will be astonished at what an invigorating effect it will have on you to let them go. The actual griefs, the bitter sorrows, the tragedies, the irreparable sense of human loss—let these go too. It does you no good to cling to these and brood over them; it does nobody any good. Let them go, and let God help you build something happy and worthwhile into your life.

In any situation, try to contemplate God's relationship to you and His attitude toward the situation. Then, boldly take over this same attitude as much as you can, definitely become a part of God, the good. Do this in your difficulties, and you will find that they have disappeared or have taken on an improved form in your outer experience. Within your own hidden, vital nature, God is renewing and rebuilding you, equipping you with the wisdom and strength to master every emergency. This is the way to live in Truth. When Truth is lived, demonstrations take care of themselves.

I can freely and effectively bless my body or any case

of sickness in another by quickening my realization of God as free-flowing life and all good. I can feel about my body just as God would feel about His materialized body and just as if my body were His own—which it really is. I can feel this same way about anything with which I am in any way concerned. I can feel just as God would feel under these same circumstances—just as He does feel—in and through my uplifted consciousness when I lift myself up to God and let God. This mighty Presence becomes a part of my self. God fills me with divine life, power, and perfection of good.

The warp and woof of our daily experience is woven of our thoughts, beliefs, and feelings toward ourselves and toward our world. We are humanly hampered by our sense of present limitations and by the ghosts of old doubts and fears. Our human instincts are often so deeply buried in us that it is difficult to rout them out into the open, to take control of them, and definitely to banish them if they need banishing. But it can be done.

Release your problem when you turn to God. Dare to say to yourself, "I have no troubles." Dare to feel that way. Remember God, the good, "I have no troubles!" If you are tired, seemingly handicapped or discouraged, remember "the one who is in you is greater than the one who is in the world" (1 Jn. 4:4). "I am with you always." A tingling, new impulse from within will enliven you into new activity. It will stir you, engross you, and make you forget your sense of trouble.

This new impetus is distinctly a thing of the mind, this Spirit. It is not so much a matter of mere determination as of uplifted mood, changed in color and feeling, carrying its own sense of inevitable follow-through. By its sheer intangible strength, this changed mood carries you over the previous mental impasse, over the physical obstacles, which for the moment you forget. The fresh, new, glad slant in your mind buoys you up, revivifies you. You give yourself over to it; your new mood of happy conviction activates you: *God in the midst of me is mighty! I cannot fail!*

It is the same situation perhaps, but there are new life, new purpose, new opportunities, new slants, new outlooks, a new spirit of optimism and purpose, practiced faithfully but never mechanically—livingly.

Every day lift yourself in your own mind, mood, imagination, sheer inner conviction. Every day do something with a sense of freedom and spontaneity, something you've wanted to do or felt you should do but have shirked because of inertia or fear. Start right now. Make a program for yourself. Every day try to do something to make life more pleasant for others, not from a sense of duty or in hope of a reward, but because of the sheer pleasure of being able to do it. Then behold how these active, happy inner states increase and grow to bless you and transform you, to transform and bless your world.

The all-wise, all-loving, all-adjusting power of Christ is now lifted in me, filling me with enduring health and strength. I trust in God and am not afraid.

Chapter X
The Charmed
Circle of God's Love

The Light shineth for thee;
The Light shineth on thee;
The Light shineth through thee,
And through thee to bless the world.

*T*his little stanza carries a charm. As you think of God's presence and power, your thought of this Presence and Power travels from you in ever-widening circles. What place is there where God is not? What can your thought touch on anywhere, of whatever nature, that is stronger than God? In the charmed circle of God's love, there is nothing to hate, nothing to fear.

If there is any condition in your life that causes you dread or worry, that seems antagonistic, that seems more than you can cope with, that arouses uneasiness, a sense of friction, or insurgent uprisings in your mind, pause and remember. Remind yourself:

I walk in the charmed circle of God's love.

I live in the midst of His love.

In my life and in my thoughts, I am a medium of God's strength and wisdom and harmony and power.

I go with the current of God's mighty love—never against.

I glorify God by letting nothing but God have power over me.

We are helped as soon as we perceive that all our conflict is really mental. Our most insistent and insidious enemies are our own reactions to human situations. God wants to give us guidance, but our thoughts are too noisy, too confused, too beleaguered with doubts, too anxious, or too selfish and stubborn to be able to hear. In effect, God says one thing only, over and over: "Let there be love." But this command, even if we catch a note of it, we often misinterpret and willfully disobey.

God's will is goodwill toward us, and God's will is for us to love. Our personal will often prompts us to fear, shrink from, resent, or combat certain conditions, circumstances, people. We do not want to love them, or do not see how we can. We draw back into our inner quiverings, impotences, aversions, rebellions. We are mistrustful, fearful. But through and under all circumstances, God tells us one thing: "Let there be love."

Spirit will help us if we sincerely seek God and let God be God. Spirit knows the way out of all human dilemmas. God is the answer.

Sometimes in the turmoil of our disorders, it seems difficult to find God, to feel sure of God, to understand how God works, and to unify ourselves with that great loving Power.

After my first marvelous healing through prayer, I was often distressed by undesirable situations in my world and by uncontrollable doubts, indecisions, and embroilments within myself. My understanding of God,

God's laws, and God's ways had increased—or had it? Sometimes I felt more inadequate, baffled, and torn than when I had first turned to the Lord.

One day, utterly discouraged, I tried to realize the Father's infolding love and wisdom. But my mind and heart were too full of other things: disappointments, fears, grievances, failings of my own and of other persons. Suddenly it was as if someone spoke to me: "Lift yourself up!"

I was startled and abashed. How sorry and mean my inner self must look to the Father—my shrunken, flabby spirit discolored by such ugly, bitter things! The voice continued: "Come to yourself! Be strong! For I have not given you a spirit of fear, but of courage and of love and a sound mind!"

I weakly alibied, "I try to realize that, Father, but everything about me keeps going crisscross and keeps pulling me down."

"Are these things stronger than I am?" the voice questioned.

"Sometimes I don't seem able to feel Your presence, Father," I answered. "The discord around me is too strong. I know that my worst enemy is the negative thoughts stored in my own heart and mind, but when they rise against me, I don't know how to deal with them."

"You don't have to deal with them," He said. "Forget them; remember Me."

I was engrossed with a long list of ills and unanswered prayers that I wished to bring to His attention. But as I started formulating them, He interposed,

"Forget them! 'Be still, and know that I am God!' " (Ps. 46:10)

A dim sense of reassurance and peace began stealing over me, as if against my human will. Then my human self tried to resume its questionings: "But Father ..."

"Don't resist! Don't you understand how you are resisting your good?"

"But Father ..."

"Don't argue! Trust Me. Trust!"

"How can I?" I pleaded. "These conditions are hard and difficult. These people ..."

"Be still!" And then: "These ugly things you are so insistent about are figments of the human mind. Why do you let them sully, rend, and destroy you? Forget them."

"But I can't, Father. I don't seem able—don't know how—"

"Peace!" commanded the Father. "There is nothing but good. Let all contentions be silenced. Let these tor-turing false images be dissolved out of existence in your world. I will dissolve them, for I am the solution. The sole solution."

In the deep hush, He spoke again: "There is nothing but My power—and My power is love. Let! Let Me!"

As a sense of His meaning spread into my mortally sick and harried soul, I felt a wave of transcendent glory—peace. Yet the inadequate, craven part of me persisted: "While I am here alone with You, Father, I feel strengthened and reassured. But as soon as I go forth into the world again, into the difficult situations that I dread ..."

"You cannot go where I am not. Wherever you go, you can take with you the remembrance of Me. Where I am, there is no dissension, no conflict, no disorder, no hate. Wherever you move, you move in the circle of My love. You must carry this thought always with you. It is your most imperative duty, your greatest blessing."

The flood of glory that poured through me then was such as I had never experienced before. Guidance, wisdom, forgiveness, steadfastness, strength—not mine but the Lord's. Wherever I moved, I moved in the charmed circle of God's love—a conveyer of His blessing!

Thank God for the day when you discover there is no enemy, no conflict, excepting that which rages in your own mind. Thank God for the moment when you realize that your most unruly thought can be brought into line. God can and will help you rule these inner tumults of confusion and strife. Your thoughts, reactions, and innermost feelings may seem to rise against your will, but consider: Is this situation stronger than the invisible but mighty tide of omnipotent love? Your own turbulent thoughts and instincts are embattled only because they are trying to buck the mighty tide. Any moment, you can bring them into line by bidding them to cease resisting and go along peacefully with the current.

Spiritual mastery is the most important battle you will ever win. It is a difficult battle from the mortal sense. Only with God's help can you win it. "Let Me!" says God. God brooks no conflict, and God wins by silencing and dissolving every rebellion and contention within your own soul. It is only after this inner victory and in proportion as we are steadfast that we can attain an abiding peace and poise within, a sense of love and wisdom infallibly controlling and directing the entire creation.

The Truth that Jesus taught is not a philosophy of life, not a creed, but a way of living. Our conscious connection with God is the important thing. But our knowledge of God and of the Truth that Jesus proved is of little value to us unless it helps us solve our daily problems. When we catch a new glint of understanding, we must apply it and use it in every department of our workaday world if we wish God to work through us and bless us.

The trouble is that we are all humanly out to "get" something, if only what we term our *rights*. We are not willing to become a means of expression for the Father through which the glorious all-providing good may flow to bless us and our world. Every inner inharmony arises from the fact that we are personally striving to "get the best of" some situation or some person. We are really striving to exert our personal will over the condition. Our self-concern, our self-importance, our almost unconquerable desire for self-justification cause more dissension and stress than any other element in the human makeup, leaping up and insistently clamoring, "Me! Me! Me!" This is the human traitor within ourselves that bars us from yielding to the will of the Father.

It requires faith and considerable practice to change our mental attitude. It helps me both in reducing my instinct to "get" and my personal sense of effort or conflict to think of myself as a channel through which God's powerful essence of love and wisdom is continually passing. It is conveying itself through my receptive mentality to be transmitted into every department of my visible world. My realization of this makes it easier for me in the spirit of sincerity, conviction, and authority to pronounce spontaneous, heartfelt blessings on adverse situations.

Try it. Bless your distressing circumstance with a realization of God's presence and power. Bless with thoughts of peace and joy the persons who have affronted you. Bless the conditions that have frightened you. Bless the needs that you have seemed unable to meet, the strangers you pass on the street. Bless even the drudgeries that you have hitherto hated. You are a channel for God. Respect and honor God by utilizing your full ability willingly and cheerfully. Feel an interest in how well the smallest job may be done. This goes for the upkeep of your personal appearance and your home too. You will be surprised at the improved results both in yourself and in those around you. You will feel better inside too. This is God's way of saying to you, "Well done, good and trustworthy slave." It is God who gives the increase, and as soon as you merit better circumstances, you may be sure that God will see that you have them.

God knows how; God is trustworthy. God always gives us the answers if we put aside our limited personal self and learn to go with the universal current. Once a very sick man was not expected to live through the night, so a Truth healer was summoned. The healer entered the sickroom and sat silently at the bedside, immersing his whole consciousness in the loving Presence and Power. Presently the sick man stirred and looked up. "Why, it is easy!" he said. "Yes, it is easy," replied the other. "I hadn't expected it to be so easy," said the sick man, dropping off into peaceful sleep. When he woke up, they knew that he was not going to die. "It is easy." Often in spasms of pain or fear, these three words have recalled me to remembrance and acted like a talisman. When we trustfully let God take charge, God does not fail.

I live in the love of God. Everywhere I go, I carry God's love with me. There is no escaping it. Sustaining me, soothing me, protecting me—yes, even from my own willful, embroiled human thoughts. Guiding me, strengthening me, blessing me, and through me, blessing my whole world with divine love and peace. I carry this realm of peace with me wherever my thoughts may travel. Wherever I go, whatever I do, I live, move, and have my being in the charmed circle of God's love.

Here is an adapted version of an ancient French prayer that expresses the creed of the one who has found the Christ way of love and loving service:

"Lord, make me an instrument of Your peace. Where there is hate, may I bring love; where offense, may I bring pardon. May I bring union in place of discord, Truth to replace error, faith where there is doubt, hope for despair, light where there is darkness, joy to replace sadness. Make me not crave so much to be loved as to love. It is in giving that one receives, in forgetting self that one finds and wakens eternal life."

The inspiration of the Almighty gives me understanding. "Not by might, nor by power, but by my spirit, says the Lord."

Love warms me with its spirit of forgiveness. My heart is warm with love toward everybody and everything; and in divine order, my mind, my life, my affairs, and my whole world are transformed. I put my faith in God's presence and power. Father, I thank You that You have broken through the resistance in my consciousness. In the boundless circle of Your love, Your glorious will is done.

Chapter XI
There Is a Place

You and I should feel grateful today, this moment, every moment of every day, for there is a place accessible to us where we may find tremendous, life-transforming help, whatever our seeming limitation, lack, or need. It is a place where we find our health and are sure of it, where we find ever-increasing happiness, confidence, ability, poise, and peace.

The negative situations and conditions that have caused you such turmoil and uncertainty are all based on fear. Insidiously interwoven into the human mind, human fear pertaining to all kinds of things and possibilities in the external world is the basis of every conceivable human ill. Human fear brings about physical sickness, injustice, weakness, poor performance, failure. There is but one way to counteract human fear and to do away with it utterly. This is simply to drop from your attention the things or conditions that have caused your dread. You cannot do this alone, the only way to do it is to become God conscious. There is a place in you where you can become aware of the living, active God, where you can give Spirit full credence and trust. This is the marvelous place I have mentioned from where seeming miracles emerge, where amazing changes take place in which you are made into a different person, in which your whole life is transformed.

God is with you!

Just how often do you think of that? What does the presence of Almighty God really signify to you as you eat and think and plan and pray and play and carry on the various enterprises of every day? Are you really interwoven with the invisible fabric of Almighty God, warp and woof, when you yield your secret soul to dreads and shrinkings and to assaults from the external world? No! You have forgotten God, what God is, and what God indubitably can do for you.

Yet any moment you so decide, you can turn innerly and learn to abide in this wonderful place where you will be rebuilt and renewed. New strength, new courage, new confidence, new energy, new purpose right where you are, under whatever circumstances, you can switch your attention to God, who is the ever-present, omnipotent Spirit of Good. You can name and claim God; in any situation, you can practice giving your full credence to the supreme presence and power of the Almighty. You can practice abiding faith, fully expecting—knowing—that God is rightly and powerfully acting in and for you and will adequately, victoriously, reveal Himself in your visible world in plenty of time. But you must yield yourself fully to the sense of the good now actively at work. This is the place of true prayer: a supreme and indestructible consciousness of God, of His love and your trust, and of divine cooperation, which you can carry with you wherever you go, into the humblest task or the highest undertaking.

It is not a question of being self-conscious or merely world-conscious, but God-conscious. God is with you. Any moment, increasingly every moment, you can feel this marvelous realization becoming more spontaneous, alive, and vivid within you. Suffusing your whole being, permeating your whole consciousness, flowing illimitably from beneath your consciousness, filling you with the sense of God, the unseen but infallible action, caring for, protecting, adjusting, and directing you and your whole world. No wonder you begin to feel better. Your human shackles, your bonds and irritations and frets and fears, whatever they may be, have lost their power over you. God is present and in charge. Let God have full sway. In the soothing, electrifying sense of God's nearness, directorship, and power, you are willing to relinquish your personal strains and bothers, your human shortcomings, your prejudices, your petty annoyances, your weaknesses and dark emotional surges, your previously engulfing hardships and hatreds and fears.

God's mighty directive wisdom and love and power are washing your life clean and pure and bright for you, are extending before you paths that are inspired—paths that are sure, undefeatable, happy, and blessed. They cannot be other than blessed any moment of any day, no matter what your mind or hands may find to do, for at the very foundation of your being, God is with you. Your sense of the Presence and directive Power in all that you say and do and function with and are, grows and spreads through your whole being. The Presence is in the midst of every thought and deed and aspiration, every physical functioning and external enterprise.

God is with you. And God is good. More and more you can feel the Presence charging your own innermost being—coloring and changing it from doubt and weakness into glorious certainty and strength. You are willing to give up your anxious concentration on ways and means, on specified results, for God's results are bound to be good. The ills of your environment become less provocative to you as you release yourself from the necessity of grappling with them personally. Your sole responsibility is to remember that God is ceaselessly with you. In this increasing realization, you can even let go feeling responsible for yourself. What a blessed relief! God becomes responsible for you the moment you cease feeling responsible for yourself. Your responsibility to God is to give yourself over to Him so completely that you feel surcharged with Him, with His ceaselessly active, illimitable, infallible good.

This place where you come to intimately feel God's loving, powerful presence has no tangible location. You can take God with you and unerringly find Him in any spot, condition, circumstance, or venture. Jesus said, "The kingdom of God is within you." We usually say that knowing God is a matter of consciousness. But the term *consciousness* seems too cold and abstract to have a vital meaning for many of us. Yet our consciousness is simply what we are aware of. In the complexities of life, there is much that we are continuously, changingly aware of in various areas and fringes of our consciousness. Our thought stream is constantly being altered and colored by things that are happening to us, by various impressions we are constantly receiving and registering, often without our being definitely aware of the shifting and change. Our thought stream is so close to us that it is often difficult for us to analyze it, to name definitely its contents or to exert control over it. But the thought stream can be controlled through vigilance and persistence, through refusing to give attention or allegiance to any power less than God. If we decide to let God rule our consciousness for us, God will help us in this task and bring it to a successful issue.

This is the place where the most important victory of our lives will be won. Our practice of the loving, infallible presence of God must be kept up until it becomes an established verity to us, not just something that we think about once in a while and frantically call on when we think ourselves in danger. If we have really found God and trust God absolutely, we know that there is no danger. For we know that God is with us, in charge of every situation, bringing forth only good—every good outcome we can conceive or desire. This blessed knowledge and all that it connotes has come to fill every whit of our conscious mind. We are the human receptacles, instruments, agents of the Almighty; we have become fit, perfected, protected channels in all that we think, aspire to, and do. This has become our habit of thought and feeling. We don't have to pump up the thought of God to rescue or to aid us. It springs to our aid and simply wipes out the fear of ill before the negative thought has had a chance to register or to make any impression. So deeply is our God-consciousness established that it has blended with all our instincts and intuitions, inclining them toward absolute trust and dependence on God. We draw on Spirit as simply and spontaneously as our lungs draw breaths from the air. We cannot doubt or dread or fear; this has become an impossibility because we are magnified in God. We cannot worry, be suspicious, or feel anger or hate. Through the practice and establishment of God's presence, we find that our attitude has changed, not only toward the Almighty but toward ourselves and our capabilities and toward the things and circumstances that combine to make up our external world.

This altered attitude of confidence, absolute assurance, joy, enjoyment, and expectancy of good can be put into the humblest task. You will tingle with a new and unguessed sense of freedom as you shake off the old dreads and inhibitions. God is with you. God is protecting, sustaining, leading you. Not only for yourself but for every associate and situation you can feel the actively beneficent Presence. Why be craven or inert or unforgiving or suspicious or mean? Better, a million times better, to thrill with the gladsome upsurge of strength and conviction: *The omnipresence of God fills my whole world with good.*

God works for us from within outward, and we cannot always calculate how divine beneficence will be manifested, except that it is dependent on full self-surrender and absolute trust. During an intense spasm of physical pain, a certain woman was trying to keep her attention on God. Prayer had helped her to endure previous attacks, and she had, to a certain extent, lost her fear that in the midst of one of them she might die. She was straining to remember that God was her life, her physical perfection, her invincible strength, but the contortions of her whole body seemed to become more violent. Suddenly she ceased all personal trying. "You gave me my life," she thought, "and put it in this body, Father, and if You want to take it away, I am not afraid. It is Your life—do what You will with it. I know whatever You do will be good." She felt first a soothing sense of peace in her full surrender. Then gradually she felt the terrific physical disturbances amazingly unknotting and smoothing themselves out. Her whole body seemed to relax and adjust itself as if under the ministrations of a great, loving, infinitely skillful hand. It must have been that insidious and perhaps unsuspected fears were touched and erased away. "I must not ever forget this," thought the grateful woman. "O Father, teach me how to trust You more and more!"

Later she carried the lesson of this experience into other phases of her life. God would work in every department of her life if she would let Him. She must yield herself to divine power and let God erase whatever obstructions there might be—discouragements, bitterness, anxieties, and petty concern for self. She had to learn human forgiveness and the true meaning of trust and love. Her health improved steadily. A partial paralysis was cleared away as if certain parts of her body had been freed at the same time that her mind was liberated from constricting fears. She tried not to entertain any thought that had previously caused antagonism or dread. She simply dropped it, remembering the presence and power of God and putting every phase of her life in God's keeping. It wasn't always humanly easy, but she must not forget.

Her health improved; her opportunities increased as well as her ability to meet them; her environment became happier; her attitude toward her associates, toward her work, and toward life was more friendly and optimistic; and one day she realized that her whole nature had changed. More resourceful, kinder, more tolerant and patient, more cheerful and courageous, more dependable, more confident of success and more successful, she had become a different person. In all her dealings, enterprises, situations, and in every small task she learned to include God by dropping the mere personal attitude. It was first a formulated prayer that helped her, then it grew into the very fiber of the being, whence it came forth spontaneously:

I am a creation of the Most High and am now open to God's fullest blessing!

And veritably in her manifest world, she walked with blessings, the most assured and dependable blessings in this changing world, for they came from the Most High.

I am lifted up to the Christ-consciousness. I am one with all love (good) everywhere. I am at peace with the world. I am free. I am free.

You build your consciousness of God's presence not only by meditation and prayer, not only by changing your thought habits and controlling your wayward emotions, but by means of the things you do all day long and through the spirit in which you do them—not strainingly, dubiously, or rebelliously, but freely, confidently, gladly. By your uplifted and gladly expectant attitude toward yourself, your God, and your world, you yourself are metamorphosed, and your outer experience is bound to change.

Remember every moment of every day that in every fiber of your being, in every contact and venture and situation, permeating, protecting, guiding, and blessing, *God is with you!*

Chapter XII
I Have No Fear

____

W hat would be about the greatest boon you could possibly imagine? Would it be to be absolutely without fear? Psychologists say that fear, deeply imbedded and of long standing in the minds of men, is at the bottom of most of the ills that human flesh is heir to. Fear among nations causes war. Fear among individuals causes hatred and violence; weak tremblings and shrinkings; vain, ostentatious pretensions; and covert, underhanded dealings. Fear causes us to live in a world of confusion and uncertainty, of desperate striving, of ceaseless battle against that which threatens to pull us down; until, finally, fear shatters the very cells of the body itself.

Ugly, destructive fear! People do not want it in their lives. But how to get rid of it? In the first place and in the ultimate analysis, it is for their very lives that humankind fears. And wedged into their life spans is the full category of other fears, big ones and small ones, petty ones and terrific ones, clouding, spoiling, and marring their chances for happiness and content. What are you afraid of? Are you sick and afraid that you will not get well? Are you afraid of the future, of the vicissitudes and insecurities of life? Are you afraid that the welfare of your loved ones is in jeopardy? Are you afraid you cannot find a job or that you lack ability to fill the one you have? Are you afraid of the world's opinion or of the moods and tempers of other people? Are you afraid that you will not get your just desserts—or perhaps that you will get them? Are you afraid of long, sleepless nights, and even more afraid of the daybreak that brings with it the necessity of carrying some decision through?

A thousand and one fears are so interwoven in the warp and woof of our lives that it would seem impossible to overcome them. Yet there is a method—Christ's method. Fear is a very human trait, but where God is there can be no fear. Then the one sure antidote for human fear is to remember our connection with God. "Be still, and know that I am God!" How many of us have the simple directness and courage of Christ? How many of us have the faith to remember God and what God stands for in relation to His creation, to put God first and keep God first in the face of every adverse seeming, to put ourselves and everything that concerns us in the Father's keeping and keep them there in an absolute fullness of personal surrender, confidence, and trust? "Not my will but yours be done," prayed Jesus, knowing the omnipotence, omnipresence, and loving-kindness of the Father. "I do not speak on my own; but the Father who dwells in me does his works," said Jesus, as He was teaching His disciples concerning the Father.

What a wonderful feeling of relief and freedom begins to steal over us once we have caught even the faintest perception of the presence and willingness of

Almighty God. God is helping us—God who is stronger than any of our difficulties, against whom nothing else can stand. How it eases us just to hand over to God our problems, all the snarls and perplexities that have been too much for us. We can feel our taut, strained nerves gratefully relax. God is here, will see us through, will tell us what to do.

We should be thankful that our minds are so constituted as to make it impossible for us to think more than one thought at a time. While we are thinking of God's presence and power, we cannot simultaneously think of our personal inadequacies, hardships, and dreads. But we ourselves must direct our thoughts toward God and establish them there. Whether we do this is entirely up to us. Even God cannot do this for us.

What we think about—the nature and trend of our thoughts—colors and directs the trends of our lives. What we react to and the way we react constitute for us the emotional structure in which we daily and hourly live. What we believe in by virtue solely of our beliefs is true for us. Whatever we think may or can hurt us can hurt us by virtue of our mere belief that it may or can! Through our own belief that it can, we give it that power. If we really believe that a thing cannot injure or affect us, if we really believe that a higher power is working for us against which nothing adverse can stand, as long as we believe thus with respect to our individual vulnerability, no adverse thing in the world can touch or affect us.

In what are you putting the strength of your belief? In the ugly, undesirable things or possibilities that are making you miserable and unhappy or in a higher power, a power transcendent of every adverse earthly seeming, a power intangible yet unfailing, inviolable? Infallible, illimitable, omnipotent! Just what does God mean to you?

It seems to me that the best prayer for any of us is the one that serves best to soothe, assure, and strengthen the human side of us. In our human needs and anxieties, we turn to the Father. "Father, of my own efforts I have failed. I now turn to You. Not by my might, Father; not by my puny, personal might, but by Your grace. Take care of this, Father." And the sense of peace that comes after this giving over is the first proof that God has heard and is answering our prayers.

You are more peaceful. Have you ever stopped to think exactly what has happened? In your mind and heart, which were formerly filled with doubt and fear, room has been made for peace. There is less room for fear. Powerful, restful, joyful, healthful, plentiful, trustful, all these are good-sounding words. They are words we should all like to feel are descriptive of us, of our inner Self. And as our minds and hearts become more and more filled with God, with a consciousness of peace and plenty and joy and power, less and less room is left for the dreads and uncertainties by which we have been previously tormented.

Whatever serves best to aid and fortify your crippled human forces is your best prayer: "I am with you always." "The battle is the Lord's" (1 Sam. 17:47). "Stand still, and see the salvation of the Lord" (Ex. 14:13 KJV). Give yourself over to the sheer, glorious comfort to be found in these assurances, the feeling that it is not your puny, human strength that is now being tested but the illimitable strength and power of Almighty God. Yield yourself. Taste and experience to the utmost the joy of your human release. *It is not I, but God.* Whatever your problem, your fear, your nagging anxiety, just hand it over. Comfort yourself with this divine assurance: *God is here. God is working in and for me. Nothing can stand against God.* Know that—feel it. The last thing before you go to sleep at night, relax and thrill to the joyous realization of it. Put everything else aside, every evidence to the contrary—every adverse evidence, every upspringing uncertainty or doubt or dread. Wake up with it, or if you waken with a gloomy pall of anxiety seemingly hanging over you, push through it and call to that thought of divine assurance and support which previously has given you peace. Call to it—call it forth.

God is here. God in the midst of me is mighty. God rules. In every smallest thing, I am relying on God. "Father, I thank You for Your unseen presence and for Your protection, peace, and power which fill my entire world."

Do not be afraid to ally yourself with God. Hand over to the Lord every thought, every fact, and condition that causes you dread and worry, that is too much for you to handle. Do not hesitate—hand them over. Know that God is regulating these worrisome matters and conditions for you now. Know this as a blessed Truth. Thrill to it. Whatever thought gives you assurance, whatever it is that assures you that the presence and power of God is now working mightily in you and your affairs, take

hold of it. Take hold of it fearlessly and let it be assimi-
lated into and throughout your being. God is helping
you now—God Himself! Almighty God, with divine
power and love and wisdom. Who or what in the world
can stand against God? Over and over send the glad
message to your tired, fretted brain cells; to the darkest,
gloomiest, most shrinking corner of your mind; to every
fraying, straining, quivering nerve of your body. Send it
again and again. God is here and is now doing a mighty
work. God is omnipotent, infallible, omnipresent—
what can there possibly be for you to fear? Charge your
mind with this glorious, freeing, electrifying thought;
charge and fill your whole being with it. It is true. It is
true for you in proportion as you fill yourself with it and
know it and feel it through every atom of your being, in
proportion as you know and feel it to the exclusion of
everything else—of every dull, dire, negative factor
opposed to God. God's will for you is good—everything
that is harmonious and right. That which is not good,
God does not wish to have come forth in your life. God
can and will bring good forth if you give Him a chance.
But even the Lord cannot bring good forth if you do not
make room for Him, if you clutter your mind, which
should be receptive to God and God's Truth only, with
doubts and ugliness and fears. Say to yourself, "Today I
will give God a chance by putting myself and my affairs
wholly and unreservedly in His hands."

Claim God's mighty help; do not delay or shrink
from it. God is reliable. Feed your mind with thoughts
of the reliability of God. Let your mind be trustful,
hopeful. You cannot go too far in picturing or conceiv-

ing the reliability of God. God doesn't care how high you build your conception of Him or how much and how far you depend on Him. God wants you to build Him to the utmost. God wants you to depend on Him. God wants to express Himself through you, wants you to be more and more a perfect expression of the Divine. God wants you to be filled to the utmost with spiritual life and love and wisdom and power. God wants these to flow harmoniously through you. God wants you to be healthy, happy, and abundantly supplied. God wants you to be undaunted, intrepid, and free. God wants you to partake of His own divine, illimitable assurance and strength. God wants to bless you.

Do not let your human doubts or timidities hold you back. Do not let the opinion of anyone in the world hold you back. Make your first claim on God in whatever terms best satisfy your individual need. Let your courage manifest itself in daring to approach and claim God, the power that works within you and that is stronger than any force that can threaten or assail you from without. Claim God; ally yourself with the Lord. Identify yourself with those divine blessings of which you feel the most vital need. Life, love, peace, joy, plenty—of these, God has an inexhaustible abundance.

I am unified with God. By my faith, I am unified with God's life and power and all the good there is.

Send the message to your mind, to its farthest corners, again and again—the last thing before you go to sleep, the first thing when you waken, a dozen times daily, a thousand times if need be. As you perform your daily tasks, as you go forth to meet a problem, build a sense of your alliance with Almighty God into your deepest consciousness. Live in the mighty omnipresence of God.

God is here. Even though results do not come instantly, be steadfast. Though outward conditions and circumstances appear unchanged, let your own changed, thrilling sense of God cooperation uphold you. God cannot fail. "I do not speak on my own; but the Father who dwells in me does his works." Be inwardly confident and serene. "The battle is the Lord's." In the face of any adverse situation or trial, say to yourself: "This doesn't matter; it doesn't disturb me. Nothing can disturb the peace of mind of God's creation." Even if calamity should threaten—and especially then—refill yourself with peace and trust. Say to yourself, "God rules, and God is working everything out just right." You may not see how God will work it out or how salvation can come to pass, but if you have filled your heart and mind with trust, you know that it surely will. You are kept calm and steady by the strength of your confidence, your inner conviction. You are filled with your confidence in God instead of nervous, panicky fears. When you are filled with trust, you trust God to disclose all the hows and whys in their proper time. You trust God to reveal to you in plenty of time what you of your own part must humanly do. And God will!

Most of us are slaves to our human conception of time; we drive ourselves desperately; we fret and moil and stew lest our deliverance arrives too late. It is when we lift our eyes and put our reliance solely in God first that we finally perceive that there are no desperate urgencies in Spirit. In God's realm of order, beauty, and harmony, there are no desperate urgencies of any nature. In Spirit, "the time is fulfilled." Remind yourself, reassure your own human mind regarding all your earthly emergencies. Live in a continuous state of divine reassurance: *I am Spirit ... Nothing can hurt me or make me sick or afraid, for Spirit is God ... God works in me to will and to do whatsoever He wishes me to do, and He cannot fail.*

God cannot fail. God does not change. No, it is you and I who must change, so as to open our hearts and our minds and make room for God, and be filled to the brim with divine good.

But even when we desire to receive God, to cast off everything else and open ourselves to God fully, it is our own minds that present the worst difficulties. The human mind with its intricacies and longtime habits and deep-rooted sense beliefs can play us such unwanted and sorry tricks. We want to believe; we want to live and have our being in the full freedom of our glorious belief, but hidden little kinks and twists in our minds keep cropping up and thrusting themselves in the way.

In the pamphlet "The Substance of Faith," Charles Fillmore has written, "The intellect grasps it [Truth] first. The next step is the bringing forth, in the subconscious, of substance and life."

We must not fight the mind and the human concepts stored away in it, because such embattlement sets up resistance and causes increased tension, disquiet, and disorder. We cannot fight the mind, but we can give it into the keeping of God. We can bless it and let the blessing seep into every nook and cranny. "Be still, and know that I am God!" We can first soothe, pacify, and assure it; then we can deliberately, patiently, lovingly do our part in building our consciousness to a fuller realization of God until God fills us, every nook and cranny. This task is not always easy. It requires vigilance, diligence, and patience on our part, but it can be done. It is done by instantly replacing every adverse or "not-good" thought with a thought of God. We have fortified and coaxed our minds along, but we must be true to God. We must no longer think thoughts that are weak, cringing, ugly, cramped, mean, ungenerous, or unkind. We have called on God for help. Every adverse, unworthy, dragging-down thought in the mind and heart must be surrendered if God is to enter in and rule supreme.

God will surely help us, but we have our own part in the matter. He created us free agents, masters of our own minds. Some years ago I read an impressive article to the effect that we are human magnets and attract to ourselves that to which we are mentally attuned. It is easy to see what a valuable lesson there is for us in this. Sometimes we get so enmeshed in and saturated with our fears and despondencies that we can attract only what is negative—more troubles and miseries. We certainly do not want to do this, and it should be a great comfort, encouragement, and incentive to us to know that it is a condition we can remedy. We can choose to tune in to what is positive, constructive, and happy, to what is uplifting; we can identify ourselves with all great, unseen forces instead of those that are lesser.

Sometimes it may seem difficult to control our thoughts and emotions, but it can be done. God will help us do it, for in every constructive, uplifting undertaking, we are really seeking to identify ourselves more closely with God. Surely it is more pleasant to ally our mental world with what is good and desirable than with what is undesirable.

Do not say you cannot do this. You can! You can identify yourself with health instead of sickness, with love instead of hate, with good cheer instead of pessimism, with good fortune instead of misfortune. Jesus bade, "Do not let your hearts be troubled, and do not let them be afraid" (Jn. 14:27). These words clearly indicate that we alone are responsible for the conditions in our heart. If you so choose, you can fill your heart with cheer, joy, hope, trust, and peace, instead of dismal fear. Persevere. Do not wait for an outer "demonstration" before you start rejoicing. In the sheer blissful realization that you are now mentally unified with every good and happy thing and in your increasing certitude that everything is working out well for you, give thanks and rejoice. Soon your mental load will lift, and you will begin to feel better. And when you feel better, when you become peaceful and poised, you do your work better, you act differently, and other persons act differently toward you. If you are faithful in your inner practice, outer benefits will surely result.

God—good—outweighs everything else, is present in everything here and now, whatever the seeming. Believe in the good; call to it, "Come out!" Call to the good, the beautiful thing of God that you desire. A cer-

tain woman who undertook to heal herself of "heart
trouble" and various other troubles through prayer,
noticed how she was weighed down with fear. Her fears
were so many and so deep-rooted that she did not see
how she could grapple with them. At first she did not
try—simply surrendered them to God. The pain of her
heart attacks led her to use as an assuring prayer: "Do
not let your hearts be troubled, and do not let them be
afraid." "I am with you always." She virtually lived with
this prayer. One day she noticed the significance of the
word *fearful*—"full of fear." She started envisioning her
heart filled with all the things that she would like to
have instead of fear—faith, trust, peace, beauty, joy, and
power. Her "heart trouble" soon became so much better
that she practically forgot about it in the other delight-
ful occupations that had come to her hand to do. It was
about this time that she noticed that her other troubles
were vanishing and that her fear had vanished too.

Fears having to do with the human self, preoccupa-
tion with this self, cause most of our troubles. It is said
that most "mental cases" are caused from various kinds
of straining, self-interested anxiety. A truly big, generous, loving, trusting, magnanimous mind never goes to
pieces. The lives of people who humanly free themselves and who fear not for their lives never go awry.
One of the most inspiring Truth stories I have ever
heard is that of a woman who had been given up to die.
She asked that her bed be rolled to a window, and she
lay looking up at the stars. A tremendous sense of the
Life and Power controlling the universe came upon her,
and she felt that she would soon be one with it, when

her Spirit presently would pass out among those stars. As she surrendered herself to the one illimitable Power, the Power itself came and flowed into her body with a renewal of life and strength, and she was instantaneously healed. Such miracles occur when we release ourselves and everything that humanly concerns us to God.

God is here—now in everything. Though your body cries out with pain, though the people around you seem cranky, events discouraging, nevertheless draw them together with yourself into the invisible but everywhere-present realm of God's love. When we pray, "God is my all; I know no fear," we gradually realize more and more deeply that God is not only our "all" but also the spiritually potential, powerful "all" of everybody else. God is all. We cannot shut the Lord out of anybody or anything. God rules supreme, but God rules in the realm of Spirit, which is everywhere existent. Even in the situation that may seem so adverse, in the people we have dreaded and disliked, in the very conditions that have caused us panic and distress, we find God and His illimitable blessings.

So do not waste time in fear and doubt but lift up your heart and your mind. Rejoice, give thanks, be generous in your outlook, be warmhearted and kind toward all people, let your every thought be a blessing. God will come forth out of the invisible and fill your mind and your body and heal you of all disorders. God will come into your environment and into all your undertakings and affairs. God will restore your whole world. You may not understand by just what process the miracle has been worked, but that makes no difference. "The Father who dwells in me does his works." When you are filled with God, with God's thoughts, God's ways, God's works, and God's blessings, there will be no room left for fear. You will be without fear.

"I fear no evil; for you are with me" (Ps. 23:4).

There is but one Presence and one Power in the universe, God, the good omnipotent.

I acknowledge Your presence and Your power, O blessed Spirit; in Your divine wisdom now erase my mortal limitations, and from Your pure substance of love, bring into manifestation my world, according to Your perfect law.

Chapter XIII
My Victorious Spirit

A re things going ill with you? Do you blame an unjust world, individuals, or the weight of unfavorable circumstances? Does the very spirit within you feel discouraged, crippled, embittered, and sore?

Then it is up to you to do something speedily. A sick body or an ill state of affairs is nothing compared to a sick spirit. A sick spirit must be restored. And no one but you can attend to its restoration, just as no one but you is responsible for its weakened condition.

You might as well admit this fact to start with. Nothing in the world can weaken or injure you unless you yourself allow it to do so. By your own negative feelings and reactions to the outer world, you have permitted your living spirit to be retarded in its development. Today—this moment—you can decide to change. Make up your mind to choose the better way, the only way for dependable security and success. Say to yourself, "This is the day." Know for yourself, from the innermost springs of your being, that you are aided by a mighty tide of invincible strength that flows from deep within you—the very power of God.

Know this until it overwhelms every opposing belief: "I have the power. More power than I know—full power.

All the power that God has is mine—God-power. All the God-power I can perceive, accept, and use. I have the power to love, think, plan, and build constructively; the power to use positively; the power to bless, to remedy, to heal; the power to strengthen, to improve, to beautify, to grow, to glow, to serve, to aid, to develop, to enrich. I have the power to know, and know, and know until the glad blessings I have evoked from God's invisible realm shall come forth into full, splendid, unadulterated fruition."

We must somehow find our strength, learn courage and staunchness, and enlarge our soul. Perhaps this is why certain trials are necessary. A worldly friend of mine once commented: "Of course we all need God. What some of us need is a kick in the pants, but doubtless that's God acting in one of His capacities." In a sense, I agree with my friend. God does not want us to be futile and despairing, but we must come to ourselves and lift ourselves toward the Father before He can help us. So if any material frustration starts us to behave as if we are God's children, it has veritably kicked us into the realm of blessings.

"Now we are children of God." What does this glorious and sweeping statement mean to you? God functions for us at the very source of our being. If you want more power, more confidence, more security, more harmony, more success, more love, you seek and find it within yourself first.

The imperative thing for you to do is to choose the kind of mental abode in which you want to live, and then with every ounce of your resolution begin building

it. Call it what you like—your state of mind, your consciousness, your character, or your spirit. It is that by
which you live, by which you will stand or fall. If it is
flabby, weak, disjointed, cramped, timid, suspicious,
ugly, or in any way unsatisfactory, it certainly needs
reconstructing, restoring. And restored it can be. God
will help you in your faithful efforts so that you can
accomplish a great deal. God will improve and enlarge
your vision, and in ways you do not dream of, God will
"bring it to pass" if only you are true to your new purpose and to every new light that you receive.

We generally try to improve our lot by concentrating
doggedly on the outer appearance of things. There are
so many aspects with which we can find fault, so many
"things" that we desire and the acquisition of which we
think would make us happier. Because we don't suc-
ceed in our outer enterprises, we often claim that we
are "unlucky"—but "the fault ... is not in our stars, but
in ourselves, that we are underlings." Within ourselves,
necessary and "righteous" alterations must be made
before our rightful acquisitions will come naturally and
harmoniously.

The condition of my spirit is up to me; the condition
of your spirit is up to you. What is this "spirit"? It is
invisible; nobody ever sees it, but it marks and colors
everything you think or say or do. In turn, it is marked
and colored by everything thought or said or done by
you. Whether it be in the "right spirit" or in the "wrong
spirit," the spirit in which you do anything is more
important than the thing you may do.

"Not by might, nor by power, but by my spirit, says

the Lord of hosts." "It is the spirit that gives life." The Spirit gives life. Your spirit and my spirit are our points of contact with the Life that animates us. It is our only possible point of union and identification with our heavenly Father. Everywhere around us, we see tangible effects of this most vital intangible, indicating whether the individualized Spirit is true-rooted, vigorous, flourishing, or whether it is drooping, tainted, famished, and bound.

The spirit in which you do any work interpenetrates, colors, and stamps the product. The spirit of any enterprise denotes its caliber. The spirit of any individual is that which shines forth in the person by which we determine character, nature, and breed. It signalizes itself in actions and reactions. It vitalizes the person or else reveals through him or her its own devitalization. In time, it sets its imprint visibly for all to see.

When you see a pinched, shriveled, careworn face, can you imagine how the spirit animating that face became pinched, distressed, and starved before the outer stamp was affixed? The spirit of some of us gets distended and swollen with our worldly estimates and prides and personal conceits. But like any balloon, it is easily pricked and deflated. When nothing is pumped into it from the outside any longer, there is nothing left inside; it has forgotten the source of its supply, hence it collapses.

Every thought you think, every belief you entertain, every emotion you foster is leaving its brand on your spirit, either to constrict, enfeeble, and mar, or to enlarge, strengthen, ennoble, and bless. Which choice are you making? Which way are you building?

It is human nature to magnify difficulties, to worry, fret, censure, and complain. Thus are brought about most of the ills that flesh is heir to. Psychologists and physicians agree that it is the individual's attitude toward his or her burden that makes it seem light or heavy. If you think your ten-pound load weighs a ton, it will bear you down.

A physician has stated that most people who are "overworked" are, more properly speaking, the victims of poor physiological habits and of even more harmful mental habits, the most preponderant and baneful of which are intense self-concern and worry. Another physician, recently returned from several years of medical research in China, declared in a newspaper interview that high blood pressure and angina pectoris are unknown among the Chinese. He and his medical associates attributed the absence of these diseases (so prevalent in our own country) not to diet or to racial characteristics, but to the philosophy of the Chinese. They do not worry.

According to these authorities of medical science, you can easily see what a poor policy it is to feel that "things are against you" or that conditions are "hard." How much poorer this policy is when you take cognizance of that mighty reservoir of spiritual power which is ever ready to supply every human need and which must necessarily "stand under" and sustain every material manifestation.

But even God cannot help us if we deny our divinity. Every time you think a negative, adverse, limited, or hostile thought, you are denying, defying, and defiling God—not that you can hurt or change God. God still loves you and wishes only for you to come to yourself and to your rightful estate, but you are the sole arbiter of your mind and personal destiny. That is why it behooves you to take heed.

Did you ever pause to consider how your spirit would look if it were plainly visible? Once I did so, and the vision was not pleasing. Since I deal with words and love words, I sought for every word that would best describe my spirit as I should like it to be. I made a sort of "treasure map" for my soul:

Staunch, sane, substantial—strong.
Happy, harmonious, healthy—whole.
Quickened, awake, alert—alive.
Unbound, untrammeled, soaring—free.
Buoyant, vibrant, resilient, grateful—glad.
Untarnished, flawless, radiant—true.
Courageous, dauntless, reliant—unafraid.
Poised, confident, assured—secure.
Useful, cheerful, friendly—kind.
Magnanimous, generous, forgiving—big.
Competent, willing, dependable—able.
Unassailable, invulnerable, undefeatable—sustained!

Place the idealized portrait of your spirit before your mind. Do not be afraid of making it too aspiring, too fine. For it is in spirit that we are children of the living God. In spirit, we are nourished by God, we are fed, we are fruitful— "by my spirit, says the Lord."

Think! It is the character, content, and complexion

of your spirit that determine the character, content, and complexion of what you are and what you do. You have innately the character and nature given you by the Father. Why make a lesser, inferior claim? For God will sustain you proportionately as you build your relationship high and staunch and true. Make your own claim and try to live up to it today. This is the day to begin!

You have the power. You have the power of choice, of exultant freedom in your newfound, constructive belief. You have God-power itself the moment you know this and identify yourself with it. God starts helping and strengthening you the moment you turn trustfully to the Divine. Then to the degree that you are steadfast, your wonderful new mental habit becomes more and more easy. You do not have to use so much personal force when you surrender your human will to the infallibility of God.

If you feel hampered, discontented, or unfortunate in any way, pause to consider: "In this place and in this situation have I given my best performance to the glorification of God? Have I claimed and used to the full the boundless spiritual reserves of courage, guidance, wisdom, love, and strength? Have I utilized my best abilities on this rather distasteful job? Have I been as willing, cheerful, friendly, and cooperative as it is possible for me to be? Have I shown myself agreeable toward the persons whom I have judged disagreeable? Have I taken advantage of every constructive opportunity that has presented itself, humble though it may humanly seem? Have I remained uncritical, uncondemning, trustful in times of apparent trial?"

Most likely, your answer to this self-catechism cannot honestly be yes. But the moment you perceive how your undesired experience has held within it spiritual blessings as yet unappropriated or unrecognized, the moment you can thank God for your new insight and consistently use a more constructive attitude in all your activities, from that moment, you will find yourself passing into better situations as you are ready for them.

Never undervalue the small opportunities, the small conquests, overcomings, healings, improvements. Some people invoke the protection of the Everlasting Arms and, then, sit back in a rocking chair and await their blessings, never bothering to change their perverse human habits. They wonder why God doesn't fulfill His promises and help them. Willfully, they close to God His only port of entry to them and further bind their hapless spirits with their personal egotisms, prejudices, and plaints. They refuse even to glimpse the Almighty much less to serve Him, love and trust Him.

No act of spiritual loyalty is too slight to be deemed meritorious. "Love Me, trust Me" is God's supreme command. This means here and now. You cannot shut God out of a single experience, cannot wait for the Lord to come under more favorable circumstances tomorrow. Now is the time of salvation. Your battle is won the moment you willingly surrender every thought of your mind, every instinct of your heart, every item of your world to His loving wisdom and directive power. "Love one another" (Jn. 13:34), bade Jesus. This means you must actually love and trust your enemies. Humanly this may seem well-nigh impossible, but "the one who is in you is greater than the one who is in the world" (1 Jn. 4:4).

Love is the one infallible solvent. The harmonizing of these "self" anxieties, contentions, and unrulinesses within your own soul will prove to be your most valuable conquest. It will help you if you remember that your "enemies" are equally children of God and that they are seeking the Divine in ways that you do not know. They want God too.

We often strive too hard in our overcomings. We pray and sincerely try, but with our tensity and sense of personal efforts, we only tighten our bonds. We do not sufficiently free our inner spirit to be augmented, aggrandized in God. "Prove me," He has invited. "My yoke is easy, and my burden is light" (Mt. 11:30), promised Jesus. Why can't we take God at His word and exchange all our "hard" ways for glad assurance through Christ in God!

Be lighthearted instead of heavyhearted. Be happy. Be trustful and loving. Be healthy and strong. Be cheerful and friendly. Be fearless, courageous, self-reliant. Be successful. Be generous, free-minded, and openhearted. Be every whit sane, whole, and sound.

The choice is ours to make. It is easy with God. Do not be afraid to stretch the threads and filaments of your soul. Claim jubilantly: *I am free! Nothing in the world has the power to bind my spirit. Through Jesus Christ, I have found the way to the Father. I am lifted up. I am one with all love everywhere. I am free!*

Give thanks for every new shred of decisiveness you find in yourself, for every ounce of right resolution and strength—it will grow and multiply in you. Thus God "proves" Himself.

God will work mightily in and for you as you loyally work in cooperation. No longer will you identify yourself with ugliness, bitterness, despair, or defeat. When you give up a thought of fear, you make room for a thought of courage. You can replace thoughts of weakness with thoughts of strength, doubt with conviction, friction with harmony, sorrow with happiness, inertia with vitality, illness with health, failure with success. Make your decision and then do it!

Live one day at a time. With every fine, beautiful, trustful thought, you are rebuilding your life constructively from its foundations. No longer do you allow yourself to maltreat and hamper your own spirit, which holds the living germ of all you can possibly be. Instead, you have chosen to reunite yourself with God's love and God's power.

Once in your timid prayers, it lent you strength to claim, "God can; God will." Now through your whole being, you send the bolder claim ringing, "I can; I will." You have chosen your identity; you have claimed your righteous relationship through Jesus Christ in God, and as the Father helped Jesus, even so will God help you. You have the power of choice—every moment of every day you have that power.

Chapter XIV
One Thing I Do

A re you afraid of something? Afraid that you will not be able to find a job or hold the one you have? Afraid that you won't be able to pay the rent, to meet the note coming due at the bank, or even to buy food to eat tomorrow? Do you feel the grip of terror at your heart, knowing not which way to turn, knowing not what next to do? There is one thing to do. There is really just one important thing to do. Trust God.

Have you quarreled with a friend? Is there an inharmonious condition in your home? Is your heart rankling under a slight or an injustice? In your hurt and perturbation, do you feel so confused, so much awry, and so unhappy that you are not certain just what to do? There is one thing to do that is all-important—remember God.

Are you ill, in physical pain? Has the doctor given you an alarming report? Have medicines failed to relieve you? Have your symptoms increased? Are you fearful about the outcome—so fearful that you don't know what would be best for you to do? There is one thing you should do quickly. Do it as quickly as you can; do it over and over; try to live in a state of doing it. Do it from the bottom of your heart, with the full strength of your body and mind. Turn wholeheartedly to God.

Are you in some minor quandary, beset by some major decision? It makes no difference what the trouble may be or what its nature—how big or how small. Remember quickly. Remember this and this alone. Know that it is the principal thing to know, the one vital thing, that it is true, and that it will somehow cover everything—that it will suffice. Remember this: God is here. God understands. God cares. God knows how to help. God can. *God will!*

Have you something to do, and you are not sure that you know how to do it? Has your confidence in yourself, in your strength or wisdom or ability, been somehow weakened, perhaps shattered? Has your courage ebbed, your energy dwindled, and is your enthusiasm low? Is your mind a tired, soggy blank, and your heart a weight in your chest because there is something very important you must do and you have lost faith in your ability to do it? Then this is the time of times to have faith in God!

God is here. You can't see or touch the Lord, but God is here. God knows. God cares. God knows how to help. God can. *God will!*

Sometimes this basic thought is all that the perplexed or tormented soul can hold onto for a while. But it is enough—God. Just God. Illimitable, infallible, omnipotent. "Omnipotent"—think of what that really means. Think of what those other words mean: *infallible, illimitable.* Just what does God mean to you? Formulate the highest and most sweeping conception of God that you can, and try to draw yourself up to this conception. Just God.

One thing: God! acting His mightiest in you and for you. Recognize God, trust God; forgetting all else, just remember God.

Oh, the indescribable, blessed relief of remembering God, of just throwing all else away—not trying to bring distressing details to God's attention—just throwing them away. God knows. God can. God will know just what to do. God will tell you—me—what to do. God is in charge, and there is absolutely nothing to worry about or to fear. God has taken charge. God cannot fail. Nothing can thwart God, nothing can stand against God.

Just throwing everything else away and throwing yourself on God—oh, blessed relief! There is nothing else in the world like it—the blessed assuagement, the comfort, the balm. And the growing assurance, which grows and pours in like a strong, mighty tide: "God will take care of it and help me. I am unified with God, and one with God is a majority. God will tell me what to do, the answer will come. All is well, for my trust is in God.

" 'With God all things are possible.' 'I do not speak on my own; but the Father who dwells in me does his works.' God! God, Lord of hosts! The One who sets the stars in their courses, who feeds the sparrow, and holds the universe in the palm of His hand! God! who loves me, who knows, who cares, and who can. God leads me. The Lord is my shepherd, and I shall not want. God guides my way. God brings me by paths I have not known. God makes darkness light before me and crooked places straight. God, loving, almighty Father, I place myself and all that pertains to me in Your care."

Yes, the answer will come. Do not doubt it. In the moment when you have thrown everything else away and simply thrown yourself on God, you do not doubt it. Hold to this realization. Every time the old harrowing indecisions and torments start creeping back, remember quickly. Remember God. This is enough. At your first glint of remembrance, your sense of trouble began dimming and falling away. You felt calmed and strengthened by just remembering the peace and strength of Almighty God, by letting divine peace and strength flow into and through you. You felt the dawn of a new personal strength and courage. Each time you turn to God, more strength and courage will come. The answer will come. As surely as the sun rises, God will help you when, forgetting all else, you remember the Lord and turn and throw yourself on God in faith, believing.

"One thing I do" (Phil. 3:13). As we turn to God more and more and seek to know God better and seek to do as the Lord tells us and to think God's thoughts after Him, we find that this phrase is a sort of magic formula. Did you ever think to yourself how wonderful it would be if you were happy—just happy?

Suppose some morning when you awake, you say to yourself:

"Today I am going to be happy. Today shall be a happy day for me. One thing I will do today: I will let this be God's day; I will consecrate it to Him, in it I will be happy."

Surely this is a meritorious resolve. Surely if life is worth living, if a single day of life is worth living, it should be filled with happiness. It is a glorious realization when we really grasp the fact that happiness does not depend on outer things, on external conditions, or on any trend of events. We are so accustomed to believing that happiness does depend on such things that it is difficult to shake off the belief, but if we can once free ourselves from it, we are gloriously free. Happiness—pure joy—is from within. It is a spiritual entity, a free, inalienable, untouchable gift of God. It doesn't depend on this or that. It doesn't have to be created. It is—as God is. It exists, together with peace, love, wisdom, and the other spiritual gifts in that realm of eternal, boundless light and life that lies back of the sense world of limitation. It exists there, free and boundless, waiting to be recognized, claimed, called forth.

When you awake in the morning, what a thrill of gratitude comes from remembering this, realizing its truth. God's joy is prepared for you, awaiting you, ready to be accepted in your heart. Call to it, "Joy! joy! joy!" Know that it is there, contingent on nothing, on no outer happening whatever. It is there, full and free, boundless, just waiting to pour forth its beautiful, golden happiness within you—to pour itself forth as spontaneously as the gladhearted song of a bird. It is there, without any effort of your human contrivance to create it. It is there, happiness and joy, God's free gift to us, God's children.

Merely by remembering, by thinking of this wonderful spiritual essence within you, you can feel it stir and can feel it begin to flow through your being like some marvelous elixir. Happiness, joy! Dependent on no outer circumstance, it is God's own gift, now and forever, your very own, and nothing can ever take it away from you.

Later in the day, human cares and problems may arise and the sense of that marvelous inflow may be dimmed, lost. But recall quickly, remember, call it back: " 'One thing I do.' This is God's day. God wants me to partake of this abounding joy. Today I will recognize and partake and be happy within—today this 'one thing I do.' " Over and over you may have to remind yourself, but if you are faithful, if you persevere, you will be amazed at the results. You will feel better. You will cease making demands on people and their behavior for your happiness. Contrary conditions will not have the power to upset you so much; you can always turn again to your invisible treasure. You will discover in a dozen pleasant ways that "the joy of the Lord is your strength" (Neh. 8:10). And there will be many wonderful results in the outer to surprise you.

A woman whose health was broken, whose affairs were in disorder, and whose courage was spent was led to play a kind of game with words. At first, she used it as a game to occupy her time and mind. She took a thesaurus and wrote down all the synonyms of *courage* that she could find. These synonyms led her to other words with related but variant meanings. These led to still others, and the first thing she knew, she had several pages filled with lists of words, words expressing different degrees and shades of meaning of strength, power, joy, light, kindness, resolve, health, harmony, beneficence, and peace. All the words were uplifting, helpful, and constructive, although many of them seemed far removed from the word with which she had originally started. But, meanwhile, something had happened. She had become so interested in her "game" that she never knew just when or how she had refound her own courage. But she had. She must have done so, for she found herself quickened and very eager to tackle her problems from a new, hopeful, and entirely optimistic angle. She found herself regaining her health and strength almost magically and, best of all, she found herself feeling actually lighthearted and happy even before her material problems had been straightened out, and these, too, soon became disentangled. "The joy of the Lord is your strength." Courage!

"One thing I do." Choose a good thing, and begin to do it. First and foremost, above everything else, admonish yourself, "I will trust God." Trust Spirit. Rely on the Lord! Resolve to yourself: "I will be happy; I will be cheerful; I will be peaceful; I will be kind." Definitely pick out the line of your experiment, and set to give yourself over to it. If you forget, if you find yourself pulled away by the tugs of old mental habit, by undesirable kinks in your daily living, don't be disheartened. Simply return and begin again. Simply remember: "One thing I do." Be faithful. Practice being faithful to this one thing with every bit of your mind and with your whole heart.

You will be rewarded.

God knows how. God can. *God will!*

About the Author

*L*ittle is known about Dana Gatlin's private life. She was born in Paola, Kansas, in 1884, graduated from the University of Kansas, and taught high school for three years. She moved to New York and earned her master's degree from Columbia University, then worked for the *New York Sun* as a reporter, feature writer, book reviewer, and editor of the book section. During this period, she became a freelance writer and published stories in the *Saturday Evening Post, Harper's Bazaar, Cosmopolitan, Good Housekeeping, McCalls, Woman's Home Companion,* and many others. More than two hundred short stories were published in all as well as two books, *The Full Measure of Devotion* and *Missy.*

Dana first heard of Unity from a friend in New York City who had been healed with the help of Silent Unity. Dana began reading *Weekly Unity* magazine and discovered the work of New Thought writer Richard Lynch.

Health problems, including a heart ailment, forced Dana Gatlin to return home to Kansas. She turned to Unity and experienced a miraculous healing through use of repeated affirmations and study. Her blood pressure dropped more than a hundred points in the space of a few weeks! When she was well, she discovered "a change had taken place in the way my mind was working, a new trend had come into my meditations.... I could summon that glorious, ineffable, comforting light of God's presence almost at will. But now it was as if I could feel that inner flood of light and the strengthening assurance of God's guiding wisdom and power merging with my more personal identity. I had the distinct feeling that God was acting because I was calling upon Him, because I was speaking. I, together with God! Partnership with the Divine! It was a thrilling and indescribable sensation!"

Dana Gatlin began writing exclusively for Unity from this point on and published some of the most popular articles ever in Unity literature. She wrote for *Progress, Unity Magazine, Weekly Unity,* and *Daily Word. God Is the Answer* was first published in 1938 and has been one of the best loved of all Unity's books. *Unity's Fifty Golden Years,* a history of Unity from 1889 to 1939, was written by Dana and published in 1939. A third book, *Prayer Changes Things* was published in 1951, eleven years after her death in November 1940.

Printed U.S.A.   33-6537-75C-10-94